THE MONSTER THAT LIVED IN OUR HOUSE

By
Evette Granger

MAPLE
PUBLISHERS

The Monster That Lived In Our House

Author: Evette Granger

Copyright © 2024 Evette Granger

The right of Evette Granger to be identified as author of this work has been asserted by the author in accordance with section 77 and 78 of the Copyright, Designs and Patents Act 1988.

ISBN 978-1-83538-301-8 (Paperback)
 978-1-83538-302-5 (E-Book)

Book cover design and book layout by:
 White Magic Studios
 www.whitemagicstudios.co.uk

Published by:
 Maple Publishers
 Fairbourne Drive, Atterbury,
 Milton Keynes,
 MK10 9RG, UK
 www.maplepublishers.com

The views expressed in this work are solely those of the author and do not reflect the opinions of Publishers, and the Publisher hereby disclaims any responsibility for them. This book should not be used as a substitute for the advice of a competent authority, admitted or authorized to advise on the subjects covered.

CONTENTS

Chapter 1 – Goodbye Sis 4

Chapter 2 – Survival Begins 1974-1975 17

Chapter 3 – I want to kill him 1975- 1979 28

Chapter 4 – Goodbye Daddy 1980/1981 42

Chapter 5 – Our Trip To France 1981 55

Chapter 6 – Build a new life 1981/83 70

Chapter 7 – Stealing, Fighting and Turning 18 1985 78

Chapter 8 – The man of my dreams 1985/1990 90

Chapter 9 – The Bank Job 1990 -1992 103

Chapter 10 – Mrs Porteous I Love You 1999 -2013 120

Chapter 11 – What the hell - just give up! 2013/2017 134

Chapter 12 – The Box 2017 / 2019 151

Chapter 13 – A New Career 2019 161

Chapter 14 – Going Back Home 2019/21 169

Chapter 15 – The Blue Lagoon October 2022 181

Chapter 16 – The Queen Dies 08/09/22 194

Chapter 17 – The Last Holiday 2022/23 201

Chapter 18 – October 7th - A very bad day 2023 215

Chapter 19 – Summing Up – A Word to the Wise 2023 219

Chapter One
Goodbye Sis

The summer of 72 was the final school term for our big sister Dorian-dory. Her leaving dance was at the high school in the big hall. She had just turned sixteen and was allowed to go to it, it was a lovely evening, still warm, and I remember it was so still, no wind, no breeze. She looked lovely. We weren't allowed to talk to boys or look at them. It wasn't easy avoiding boys as they were everywhere, we did our best by keeping out of sight, or if we were in the street with other kids, we would avoid talking to the boys or interacting with them in case we were seen. If we got caught, we would probably not be allowed to play outside the garden gate for ages, so we were very careful.

According to Dad, Dory was late coming back from the dance, he knew how long she should take, to walk up the road from the school and went out looking for her. The dance finished at ten, and it's about a 10–15-minute walk to the house. He saw Dory walking up the road with a boy, nothing else, just walking and talking. He was enraged because she'd defied him. He told the boy to go home and pulled my sister forcibly up the road, telling her she could pack her things and leave the house – tonight! We knew there was trouble brewing but didn't know to what extent until we heard him say,

"Get your things and get out!"

We couldn't understand why Dory had to leave, and we heard our mother say, *"You're throwing her out because she spoke to a boy?*" she pleaded and begged him to let Dory stay, but to no avail, he wouldn't let her, he was the boss the big cheese, and we were little mice he controlled. We were all crying.

We couldn't believe this was happening; our sister was leaving, chucked out like a piece of rubbish. There was nothing we could do but help her to pack. We loaded our bogie, a sort of trolley, homemade from wood, pedals from a bike and some string. In those days, if poor kids didn't have it we just made it ourselves. We packed the bogie with her belongings and walked her down to our grandparents' house. Our grandad only lived down the road, he was my mother's father, and Dory would live there from now on. Grandad was a lovely man. He was always kind to us. We knew she'd be ok with him. We were the ones that should be worried about ourselves and mum because we were the ones that had to go back to the house where the monster lived. Dory had escaped the house of horrors, but we couldn't. I was only seven, my sister Shaila was five, and our brother Cameron was three. Little did we know after that night, there was much worse to come.

1972-1973

The next day, it was quiet in the house. We were all sad, We knew the reason he gave, but it didn't make sense because all our friends were allowed to talk and play with boys but not us. Maybe he didn't want any grandchildren, I don't know, but one thing we did know for sure was if you stepped out of line with him it would not benefit you at all. I think we learnt how to be cautious at that time. Even at the ages we were, we understood. As the days rolled by, Dory settled in at Grandad's she got herself a job in the sausage factory and in just a few months, she found herself a boyfriend from Dunfermline. It was quite far away, we had to get two buses and go over the famous Forth Road Bridge to get there and we loved that. It was a bit of excitement for us poor deprived kids, a break from living on a knife edge. We loved Dunfermline town, there were several shops, a couple of cafes and restaurants, three or four pubs, and then there was The Glen, a beautiful space full of greenery and flowers with a stream running through it. We went there often and had a picnic or just ran about playing games, it was a place of safety for us because he didn't know Dory's address although he knew she was in Dunfermline. We often escaped there when things got too bad or when my mum was scared for her life, it was our little paradise, a place we hoped he would never find, and he never did.

Dory left our family home in early September. It was the end of the summer, and autumn was on its way. I don't know when or even why it all started with him. Mum said he was all right until his father died. Then, almost hysterical, he lay on top of his father's coffin and sobbed. His brother had to pull him off; he must have loved his father a lot. His father was a pig just like him, he wasn't a good person, but his mother was a nice woman and hated what her son had become. It wasn't long afterwards that the possessiveness, jealousy, paranoia and gambling started. Dad would get angry when he lost and we all suffered. He also drank, not to the extent of being an alcoholic but he liked to get drunk, and that was when most of the arguments and violence would occur. We were living on a knife edge with a compulsive, selfish, gambling, violent drunk.

The change in our father was a rude awakening for us because he had been a good dad. But he changed and started hitting our mum. He was 6 feet tall, and she was only 5'1. Dad had black hair and so did she. Mum was small and voluptuous, and he was tall and skinny which he hated. He would put on about three vests and two T- shirts under his shirt to make him look bigger. Mum said when they first got married, every night he would undress in the dark because he didn't want her to see he was wearing all those layers under his shirt. He wore platform shoes so he could look taller. Men as well as women wore platforms in the 60's and 70's and Dad always wore a suit, shirt and tie and combed his hair back like Elvis, using Brylcreem to give it shine and hold it in place. He looked nothing like Elvis, he had a nose like a Native American Indian, but he looked more like Sitting Bull with a quiff!

Mum was a beautiful young woman, with a good complexion and a nice bone structure, she had massive boobs and a small waist she was quite thin in her early years before having us four. She gained a few pounds over the years but she was still gorgeous, a sought-after woman, we were to find out later on. We didn't see her real personality because she was quiet and lived in fear and poverty, not knowing what tomorrow would bring. She had to do all the thinking, the screaming, the hiding, the lying, the worrying, the crying and had to look after us. She was in a vortex with no escape and we were there with her. This man we called dad was turning into a monster and we were in his lair. It was tense and scary but we had to just get through it. What else could we do, living under the reign of a cruel dictator.

In mid-November 1972 the next event was Christmas -- something to look forward to. We usually had a good Christmas, Mum was the one that went to work most of the time, Dad didn't like working much, so he didn't, he swapped the roles with Mum and made her go out to work. She said she was glad to go to work because she didn't have to put up with him for a while. He was the one looking after us and did the housework, he did like the house to be clean and tidy, so we weren't allowed to leave clothes lying on the floor or toys lying about. Dad liked us clean so we would have a bath once a week and the rest of the week before bed he would line us up in the kitchen to get washed at the sink where he would wash us down with soapy water and a sponge.

He would scrub our ears and the back of our necks and sometimes he was a bit rough, depended on what mood he was in, - usually a bad one. We didn't ever get any love from him, no cuddles and kisses, no bedtime stories no learning except for how to change a plug and put a light bulb in which did come in handy later on in life but wasn't much good to us as children, as he was always there to do those things. That was his legacy, teaching us those two things be we also need to add teaching us how to hate, how to lie and be violent and live in deprivation.

That's what our upbringing was, a house devoid of love and kindness instead full of fear and uncertainty. This was the situation with him , I hasten to say, because mum was loving and caring. I remember her hugging us and telling us often that it would be alright, although I think we knew it wouldn't be.

Sometime before this night, in the middle of November we were well aware of the kind of man he was turning into, he was a bully, a Doctor Jekyll and Mr. Hyde. We could hear him saying to Mum that she wasn't telling him the truth about other men she had been seeing and demanding to know who she was sleeping with. It was all in his stupid head, of course. She wasn't having an affair and never had. It would have been impossible - she had three kids to get back to and a mad mental husband. She wasn't allowed to talk or look at any man, anywhere or at any time, just like us with the boys. Dad kept telling her she was a slag and other horrible things, just putting her down regularly between the mental torture and the beatings. It must have been so hard to carry on but she did, for us. It was the same for us children because he was mentally abusing us, too. We couldn't think or behave like children. All we could think about was whether Mum was going to be alright or not. Would she be peeling the potatoes at the sink, humming a tune or crying or beaten up, when we got home? In truth, we didn't know if she would be alive or dead when we came back from school. We didn't learn much at school, well what child could with all that turmoil, fear and sadness in their minds. Children that grow up in that kind of environment can't concentrate on anything else but what's going on in their home and the fear they have for their mothers. It's a tragic situation and kids shouldn't be left in that environment. If Mum and Dad went out dancing or anywhere really, she had to look down at the ground or at him because if she looked in any other direction he would accuse her of eyeing up other men. She couldn't even look or talk to any of his friends because he would accuse her of looking at other men. She learnt to follow the rules after being brutally attacked a couple of times. She backed down and did what he told her.

One night he had been drinking in the afternoon and got home in the early evening. We'd already had our dinner and were ready for bed. He was drunk and not in a good mood. I heard him shout at Mum,

"*You better tell me the truth!*" He kept going on about the truth while Mum said, over and over again.

"*I haven't been seeing anybody else!*" but he just kept at her, asking her over and over and her reply was always the same

"*I won't own up to something I haven't done! no matter what you do!*" I heard her shout back at him.

He turned his attention to us, asking if we knew who she was seeing. We were as bemused as she was, I mean how would a seven, five and three-year-old know if their Mum was seeing someone else? When we went to the shops, we only went to the shops, there was never any men or anybody else in the house and in any case, she had no time for affairs she worked most of the time and when she wasn't working she was looking after us, so it was all an invention of his sick mind. Even so, he went on to ask us about these affairs and all we could say was we didn't know anything. By this time he was raging and he went to the kitchen and returned with a piece of rope and an axe. He was fuming that none of us were saying what he wanted to hear.

He grabbed my brother's hand and tied it to a little solid wood stool we had in the living room and towered above him. He turned to Shaila and I, yelling,

"Tell me who she is seeing or I'll chop your brother's fingers off!"

We were sitting on the chair holding each other, horrified at what was going on and all we could say was we didn't know anything. But that wasn't good enough so he swapped Cameron for Shaila and tied her hand to the stool and said,

"You know don't you? Who is she seeing?"

Shaila wailed that she did not know, so he raised the axe,

"I swear to God I'm going to chop off your fingers!" he bellowed.

Shaila was shaking and crying, we all were, it was a terrifying experience to go through, your father, your own flesh and blood turning a normal day into a horrific nightmare. It was cold and stormy that night with heavy pouring rain, Mum was crying and screaming at him *"Don't do this! don't do it!"* She was shaking and trying to distract him.

Mum tried to plead with him,

"They're only young children, how do you expect them to know anything past what toys they want to play with?" she said. *"Even if I was having an affair, the kids wouldn't know about it!"*

Dad raged back at her, *"But you are having an affair and they must know about it!"*

Dad was convinced and all the crying and shaking didn't deter him at all . Mum finally pulled him away and he let Shaila go. Next Mum picked up the stool and whacked him over the head with it. He fell to the floor, knocked out and she told me to run down to the end of the street to the phone box and dial 999 and tell the police what has happened.

"Hurry!" she said, *"God knows what he will do when he wakes up!"*

The police appeared a few minutes later and when my mother told them what he was threatening to do and what she had done to stop him they were going to arrest her for assaulting him with the stool. That's the response we got from them even after she told them what he was threatening to do to us children. In fact the police were called to the house many times by me and sometimes the neighbours. Dad didn't care about the whole street being able to hear them arguing and then shouting and him swearing at my mother while she was screaming because he'd be rag-dolling her around the living room and slapping her. Then the punching and kicking started, all because he had a fucked-up head.

They told him that he shouldn't have threatened us and if he did it again he would be arrested and with that warning, they left. Dad was raging, so he told us to go to bed and then he beat Mum up again. We had to listen to it as we had many times in bed, we heard him slapping her in bed, saying to her,

"Tell me what you've been doing and who you've been doing it with?"

It was like a fucking broken record or groundhog day, it was a never-ending nightmare.

It was not long till Christmas now, something to look forward to. Just like all the other kids we'd have our big present and several small ones and a couple of selection boxes. We loved the selection boxes because you got all that chocolate in one go. It was amazing for us because we didn't see many sweets or chocolate throughout the year, as we had very little money most of the time, certainly not enough for treats. We would savour the chocolate bars and hold on to them as long as we could. We never knew when his next big win would be. Mum would always try to give us something sweet after dinner, she would make a milky pudding out of a packet called Angel Delight. When the contents of the packet were mixed with milk it turned into a smooth creamy strawberry pudding and we loved it. Mum also made creamy baked rice with meringue topping and custard with banana in it.

We hardly saw any fruit, except for bananas, which we always had. We would often get one before we went to bed if there was nothing else. Funny, nowadays, I'm not very keen on bananas! I wonder why? If Dad won on the horses, he'd give us money for the ice cream van when we were smaller, but as we got older he would give us two pounds and then it would go up to three, four and then eventually we got a fiver each - that was the ultimate - a whole fiver, each!

Getting that money came at a price, as most things did with Dad. My mother put on the bets for Dad. He would make her run down the road to the bookies to put them on three or four times a day. The bookies wasn't just down the road either, it was down a big hill and then over the road. Mum wasn't a runner nor was she athletic so she struggled to run up and down three or four times a day. She would be peeling potatoes for the dinner and he'd shout to her to go down to the bookies only leaving her minutes before the races began. If she was too late to put the bet on, there would be hell to pay. I know she was too late a couple of times and she just hoped and prayed that the horse wouldn't win so he would have no winnings to collect. Then one day she missed the start of the race and the horse won. She must have been terrified because she couldn't tell him she missed the start of the race. He went down later on to collect the winnings that weren't there.

We were coming back from the shops Mum was loaded up with shopping and we kids had a bag each as well. The shops were in the same place as the bookies so it was down and up the hill again with the heavy bags of shopping. Dad never did any shopping it was always Mum who had to carry the heavy bags.

We were halfway up the street when we saw him appear on the other side of the road - raging. We all met at the gate and he said to her, "*You get in the house and you lot stay here!*"

They went through the front door and as soon as the door was shut we could hear him shouting at her and saw, through the door's glass side panel, him beating her up. There was a curtain on the door and it was flapping about with every strike. It was horrible to witness. We were holding on to each other and crying. We were still very young. The next day Mum had a black eye and a bust lip and looked dazed and fed up. I think we probably looked the same.

Dad's gambling had a massive effect on us because when he lost he got angry and then he'd drink on top of the anger, which was never a good thing. Most of the violence occurred when he was drunk. He wasn't an alcoholic because he didn't drink all the time, he drank when he lost a bet, if he had any money left, or if he won and he had money to go out with when he would come home quite happy. We would always be in bed when he came in because Mum didn't know what kind of mood he would be in so it was safer for us to be upstairs. Whilst he was out we had a bit of freedom to just be ourselves and see Mum in a more relaxed mood. That was when we had the electric on because sometimes when he lost at the horses and was going out he would start an argument, take the main electric fuse out and take it with him and we would be left in the dark for the rest of the night. Not so bad in the summer but in the winter the house was dark the whole night. What he didn't know was the light in Mum and Dad's bedroom would stay on so we had one room that had a light on and the glow from the coal fire in the living room. We would make toast on the fire and have that before we went to bed and that was when we invented hide and seek in the dark, it was great fun. We would play and have our toast and make the most of a bad situation.

The pubs closed about 11 0'clock in those days. The pub was next to the bookies so Mum knew it would be about 11.30 when he staggered back up the road. We kids would be bathed and fed before 10.30 ready to jump into bed any time after that. We couldn't take the chance of him finding out about the light so Mum would keep look-out for him at the bedroom window so she could put the light off, we would run to bed and she would get into her bed and hope and pray that he wasn't still in a bad mood. We would all be silent and the door handle would turn and we'd hear the door open and close worried about what was going to happen next. It was a familiar pattern of our childhood.

The times he came home in a bad mood would be the nights he would attack Mum - the same old shit - who she was seeing? We would be kept awake until 2 in the morning but we still had to go to school the next day.

Most of the time we were at school we were carrying a heavy burden. When you have this going on for a long time it affects your mind even when you're a child, it's probably worse because kids can't do anything and they can't say what they think, not to adults anyway. You're in a vortex that you can't get out of because you have no defence. I asked my mum why she put up with it all and she said, there was no help in those days, no social workers, no women's aid or refuge only the police and they did nothing, not once was he charged and the police came a lot throughout the years but they were hopeless bastards, they obviously thought it was alright for a 6-foot man to attack 5'1 woman. Mum had to go to the hospital a couple of times and still nothing was done. So no one was going to help us, no authorities, no family, no friends no goddam God but I'm quite sure the fucking devil was living with us.

Two years had passed since Dory was thrown out of the house. It was the summer of 1974 the broken record was still playing, accusing, bullying, beating Mum up asking the same old questions. It got worse for us as he still hadn't grasped the fact that we were still just kids. We were still being psychologically tormented and Dad even thought of another way to make us talk, he decided that the man of God would make us tell him what he wanted to know. So one night he decided to take us down to the local minister's house. He knocked on the door, the minister answered to find a tall maniac and three bewildered children on his doorstep. Dad explained why we were there. The minister invited us in and said he'd speak to us.

He took us into a room, separately and asked us if we knew anything about what Dad was saying. Of course, he got the same answer - we don't know anything, we haven't seen anything. The minister told him that we told him just that and that he believed us. I mean what nut job takes his own kids to a minister's house to make them tell the truth about something they know nothing about? I think that, as mad as he was he must have realised that was the truth, we knew nothing but he still wouldn't let it go. He took us down again, twice. The second time, the minister asked us the same questions and got the same answers. The next time he took us down the minister refused and told him not to come back and he didn't. Dad wasn't even religious although there was several bibles in the house because we were sent to Sunday school and we had a bible each. I'm sure there were more than three bibles as he'd burn a bible now and again saying if he burnt a bible my mother would go to hell. I don't know how that was going to work because it was him burning the bible, but in his mad head, it must have made sense!

One Christmas Dad bought us a little white poodle. We were so happy to get the little dog, she still had her puppy coat on which wasn't curly at this stage it was a long carpet of fur. She looked nothing like a poodle just a little fur ball. As the weeks passed the baby coat fell out when you brushed it and eventually she had a full body of curls. She was still cute and we loved her loads, but as usual there was a price to pay for any little time of happiness and Dad started using our little dog as a bargaining tool.

He would come home drunk and angry and fill the bath up and threaten to drown her, He never did but it was frightening as we lay in bed listening to this and scared that he was really going to do it this time. He didn't drown the dog but he drowned newborn kittens. We had a few stray cats come to our door. Mum and I were talking one day and she told me that her mother said she would like to come back as a cat when she died and we've had several cats turn up at our doors, even when we move to other houses, at least one will turn up, how strange is that? My mum's mother died at the early age of 62, and the cause was cancer. Mum was only in her late 20's She loved her dearly and she was a good mother to her.

Chapter Two
Survival Begins 1974-1975

With Gran gone Mum had lost her support and she had to deal with her death at the same time living with that bastard. Our grandad looked after us from time to time when they were both working and he was alright, even if he was a bit grumpy. Grandad knew Dad was a compulsive gambling, drinking, wife-beating interrogator because we'd had to flee to his house several times over the years. I remember sleeping on the couch listening to one of those gold wall clocks that had gold shards for hands, on a round gold face. It tick-tocked through the silent night but at least we had peace to sleep, no shouting or screaming, no interrogation or hearing my mum crying. Grandad's was a bit of a sanctuary for us as he had quite a big garden at the back and there was a big tree there where we could climb and swing. We could be children again there and have a little pocket of happiness.

Grandma had always helped Mum out with money, if she had it. Money was very scarce in those days, not a lot of people had any and there wasn't much work in the seventies. Dad would lose all the money on the horses and if there was still a race to go he would send Mum down to borrow a couple of pounds of my Gran, telling her to say it was for food for us. Sometimes it was needed for us but he still put the bet on. If he won we'd get fed, if he lost, we wouldn't, we would get something but it could be as little as bread and jam or a fried egg on a slice of toast and a banana, before we went to bed.

This situation got out of hand, Mum borrowing money then struggling to pay it back and she always did pay it back, whether from her wages or social money. Dad knew it had to get paid back but his betting was the only thing that mattered to him, not us, not Mum, only fucking horses every weekend. He would even wait outside the whisky bond that Mum worked in, on payday and demand she give him money. Mum would tell him that he could have a little as she needed most of it for bills and food. He would accept that but always ended up with more because he forced her to hand any money she had left over and when that was gone she had to go to get a loan from Gran.

Mum left the whisky bond. I don't know why but it would have had something to do with him because she ended up leaving all her jobs because of him. When she finished work some days he'd be waiting outside for her to make sure she wasn't talking to other men, or he'd just shout out at the gate where all the workers were coming out,

"If you know Beth Granger she is married to me but she is having affairs with other men she's a slut."

Mum said when he did things like that, the other workers used to say to her.

'Is your man mad or what?"

She would reply, *"Yes he is."*

Dad was a ruthless man and selfish, which doesn't wash with me. I can't tell you how much I hate selfishness, it's not the way to be. I can't respect selfish people, why would I? They're not worth knowing and I even say it about my own family. I've got some family that are very selfish. I won't name them, but I'm sure they know who they are. I know who I am and that is unselfish and Shaila is the same. We'd give a tramp the coat off our back, we are always giving money out to homeless people everywhere we go and I'm not talking a few coins, and we've helped out family throughout the years. But Dad, he would sell the coat off his Grannies back to get money for a bet and probably rob the homeless of the few coins they had, for the same reason. He was so selfish and unreasonable that one day he put all the dishes in the sink and smashed them with his 'friend' the axe, because there was no money for the bookies. He also sold some of the furniture so he had money for the weekend's racing. This is the kind of shit we had to put up with, time and time again,

When mum left the whisky factory she went to work in the beer factory. Both these factories were in Edinburgh so she didn't have to go far and in those days firms put on work buses for the staff. I worked in the whisky bond in Dunfermline and we got a free bus to work and back and free meals throughout the shift. It was hard work but it was well paid and you were treated well enough. I can't say the same about the job I've worked in for the last 23 years in the public sector! It pays well if you work nights and weekends because you get more money for those shifts. To stay awake working all night is hard and painful and working every weekend, you can't have a social life, but I've just plodded along over the past 23 years. A lot of people I work with are lazy bastards and get away with it, and if you say anything about them being lazy bastards, you're in the wrong. How does that work ?

All I can say is, if you're a lazy bastard and you know who you are, why don't you own it? if you're not a lazy bastard then you would want to own that wouldn't you? Your selfishness doesn't go unnoticed as people talk about how they hate working with you. Any kind of selfishness is a major problem in societies. I don't know why people are selfish, I'm the complete opposite, usually to my detriment.

Shaila and I have helped family and friends out several times - what can you do when someone needs help and you're in a position to help? This includes stray cats and rescue dogs. For years we've had a lot of animals and have rehabilitated ones that needed it. This has cost us a small fortune. Our last rescue dog died about 4 years ago and we're not getting any more because with the cost of the vet bills, we just couldn't do it anymore.

I've got to say that if you're living with the male of the species and they don't help about the house and leave it all to you, they don't wash a dish or vacuum, can't even put their dirty clothes in the washing, (but then, why should they, when they've got you to do it?) It's fucking pathetic if a human being, whatever sex they are, is still breathing with their limbs working and are just as capable as I am, so there's no excuse. What I've got to say about men who show disrespect to their women, whether it's about the housework or other things men seem to think they're exempt from many aspects of life is, do these guys really think their wives and girlfriends love them for this? Well, news flash, they don't. They start to despise the other person and it chips away at them day by day week by week month by month and before you know it years have gone by and most women can't stand their men and would rather not be there, yet they don't leave. Why waste your time with these men? Don't stand for the bullshit and early on in a relationship if you see red flags, tell them, change or I'm leaving and if they don't change – leave! don't give them the best years of your life being a slave or a punchbag.

I might sound a bit bitter about men and I am, because nearly every man I've met is a useless piece of shit. I'm not condemning all men but once again if the cap fits then you should be man enough to wear it.

The weeks of our childhood rolled by another Christmas passed and we were heading into the summer of 1974. Nothing has changed, Dad 's still asking the same questions and receiving the same answers, he's still beating Mum up in bed and I was still running down to the phone box to phone the police. The times Mum shouted for me to phone the police were when she was really scared that he might not stop or would actually kill her. I would jump out of bed, put my slippers on quickly and run down the stairs, two at a time and out the front door. It was a race because he would be hot on my heels most of the time and would often capture me before I reached the phone box. He'd be in his Y fronts because that was what he wore in bed and had no time to put his clothes on. He chased me down the road, usually after midnight and I would run as fast as I could to try and reach that phone box before he did. I don't know if any of the neighbours saw us run by their windows at that time of the night but it would have been a sight to see, a father chasing his daughter in her pyjamas down the road in his Y fronts, God knows what they'd be thinking, I wanted the police to come and take him away forever, but that was not to be as he caught me most of the time and the other times if I managed to phone them, when they turned up, they didn't do anything, labelling it a 'domestic'.

In later years they said they wouldn't intervene at all. I thought assaulting your wife and terrorising your kids was against the law but apparently, in those days, it wasn't because it was allowed to go on in our house, for seven years. It was usually tense in the house because he'd be ok one minute and a bastard the next. Luckily we had a good-sized garden and we had two huts in it. A small one had been built first but was only big enough for the garden tools and a bit of storage. The other he built a couple of years later, for us to play in. It was great and there was a big shelf at the back that we could sit on. We put a curtain up and used it as a seating area for the plays that we used to make up. The plays were mainly inspired by films or cartoons we watched on the TV when we finally got one, (a small black and white one,) but it was better than nothing. I remember the first cartoons we watched were Bill and Ben the Flowerpot Men and Andy Pandy and then when we got a colour set we had the Wombles, Bagpuss and the Clangers.

They were all simply made cartoons but we loved them. Cartoons helped us escape, just for a little while and let us just be kids again. It was just a little bit of escapism whilst we were riding a never-ending storm.

We would make up games to keep ourselves occupied and sane. We invented a game called, *'blow the tissue paper to the door'* utilising the floor, the front door, a piece of tissue paper and a draft. On a windy day when there was a good draft from under the front door, we'd get the tissue paper and lay it on the floor at the other end of the hall. We would lie on our bellies and blow the tissue towards the door where the draft would blow it back. The object was to beat the draft and your opponent. The first tissue that touched the door won. It was a good game and we had loads of laughs playing it. We also had outdoor games too like skipping with long ropes, that kept us fit. Then there was accelerated rounders, a good physical game. We didn't have a bat or a ball so we used a football and our fist as a bat, we loved it and would play for ages until we were knackered.

Summer had gone, once again and autumn had arrived, it was nearly Christmas again. Christmas was the highlight of the year for us. We never went on holidays during the summer so the things we got excited about were Christmas and Easter. We would look forward to the summer because we were off school for six weeks and it was good weather. We did go on holiday once when Dad had a big win on the horses, probably the summer of 74/75, we were all still pretty young. Dad drove all the way to Blackpool with us and Snowy the poodle. We arrived quite late, about 5pm. There was no accommodation booked so we drove around a lot of B&Bs but they were either full or didn't want Snowy to come in so we had nowhere to stay. Dad's solution was for him and Mum to go to the pub, she didn't want to, but he made her while we stayed in the car. We hadn't had any dinner and we were to sit in the car for God knows how long. We got bored in the car so we decided to go over to an arcade across the road. It's a busy road along Blackpool's front, it's over a mile long with buses, trams and cars passing but we dodged the traffic and got over safely.

The arcade had loads of slot machines and games, we had never seen anything like it. We could smell food cooking and we were starving so we thought it would be a good idea to try and bust some money out of one of the penny drop machines by banging it and wobbling it to get some coins to drop. Of course, this was a terrible idea as there were people everywhere and someone came and chased us away. Some holiday this was turning out to be! It was dark now, so we went back to the car. A couple of hours later Mum and Dad came back with fish and chips, so we had our food and he said we'd have to go home as we had nowhere to stay. He had been drinking but still chose to drive 204 miles home, he kept on falling asleep at the wheel and Mum had to stay awake to make sure she could wake him up. We kids slept most of the journey. Miraculously we got home in one piece.

Mum had a lot of jobs throughout the years. Before she went to the beer factory she worked in the sausage factory, biscuit factory, whisky bond and then the beer brewery. She had to leave most of her jobs because if there was no money for him and his betting he would make her put in her notice which was only a week in those days. If she had been there for a few months she would have some holiday pay added to her payout, as well. The money was into one hand and out of the other. Mum would keep some for food and had to give the rest to Dad for betting and then start to look for another job before the money ran out. In the sixties and seventies you could do that, there were so many jobs, you could leave a job in the morning and have a new one by the end of the day! I've had 33 jobs in the past, and I hated most of them.

The job I do now I've been doing it 20 years, although I cannot reveal what that is. Everything about our childhood is true but beyond that, most of the story is true with some adjustments made to things that have happened. When I've made enough money to give up my job, I'll be able to reveal what I've done for the past 20 years.

When mum got the job in the brewery she was invited to join a money-saving scheme called 'the manage'. How it worked was that if you joined and paid into it every week, you got £60 three times a year. This money was a lifesaver. Dad knew nothing about it, which meant Mum had money at all times. Once she had her first payment she didn't need to borrow money from Grandma because she had that money that she could use. If he told her to borrow money she would go down to her mother's and just sit and have a cup of tea with her then produce the money out of her secret purse, telling Dad that she had borrowed it.

She always got it back and put it back in her purse. She had to use the money for shopping in between paydays and told him she'd had to borrow it, so that also had to be paid back. Mum was managing to hold onto most of the money, it's just as well because things got progressively worse and the money was handy when we needed bus fares to escape or if we needed food. When we went to Dunfermline there would be four fares to be paid for twice as we had to get 2 buses there and back.

There was also extra money coming in for the beer that Mum stole from the brewery for Dad to drink and sell to spend on the horses. Mum wasn't the only one doing it, others who worked there did as well, hiding a couple of cans or bottles in their knickers each shift. Mum stole so much we had a cupboard full of it. It was being sold to neighbours and to Dad's friends. Dad would drink some of it when he had no money to go out.

We were a bit better off then, but Mum was taking a massive risk and Dad was just sitting back and reaping the benefits. In those days the empty bottles were worth a few pence each, like juice bottles. Shaila and I would be sent down to the local grocery shop with juice bottles to buy bread or bananas or a tin of beans. The shop was called Browns because Mr Brown owned it. He had very little to sell, probably two or three tins of stuff but never a full shelf of anything but he seemed to scrape by. Beer bottles were also worth a few pence. We would be sent down with empty beer bottles to the pub next door to the bookies. We would knock on the door and wait until somebody came to the door usually one of the drunk punters. I would have been about 8 and Shaila would be about 6 years old. I remember thinking that these men were like giants peering down at us as we stood with the empty beer bottles in a carrier bag. We didn't like taking them down but Dad made us and it gave us much needed money for food.

The men would take the bag in and bring the money out to us and we would take it up to Dad. We hated going to the pub, it was scary and embarrassing but we went there regularly.

Christmas had passed and we got our usual presents, a main one and several smaller ones like games and toiletries and of course the eagerly awaited selection boxes. Our

Christmases were normally quite good, with Christmas dinner time playing with our toys and later watching TV. Dad would do what every other man would do on Christmas day, he went to the pub and came back about 3 pm, had his dinner and fell asleep. That gave us peace to enjoy the rest of the special day. Boxing day was business as usual, the horse racing was on and of course, he would be betting.

In 1974 I was 9 years old but felt older, maybe it was because it was hard to be a child in the house especially when he was there, which was nearly all the time. It didn't seem fair that we had to have a nightmare father indoors, most of the time, while all the nice Dads were away most of the day, working.

We played outside, weather permitting. Luckily we had a big garden at the back and a smaller one around the front. We loved autumn when the temperature started to drop, the trees started shedding their leaves, the summer flowers all died off and the days got darker. It's a really beautiful time of year, so colourful even when everything is dying off.

It was New Year's Eve, Hogmanay we call it in Scotland, with 1974 ending and 1975 starting at one minute past twelve. Some years Dad decided to decorate the living room but left it to the last minute so he and Mum would still be hanging wallpaper up on Christmas Eve and then they'd have to hang the decorations up, get us ready for bed and then wrap a whole load of presents up. Mum must have been shattered. I'll give him his due, Dad got up about 4.30 and backed the fire up so it was on for us getting up. Like most kids we'd get up around 5.30 hoping Santa had been. We would run down the stairs and burst into the living room and there it all was! A blazing fire and three piles of presents from Santa. Paper ripping and checking out each other's presents and arranging swaps took over. Christmases were usually peaceful for us as there was no racing on Christmas day so that wouldn't put him in a bad mood.

I can't remember him causing any riots at Christmas but on Boxing Day there's racing on so that could be different. I don't really associate any bad feelings or memories with Christmas trees or tinsel. New Year's Eve was normally quiet as well, as he didn't like people coming to the house, so nobody did. Mum would still do some sandwiches and cakes and the shortbread, everyone had shortbread for New Year. She knew nobody would be coming to the house but she still made the effort. In those days musicals and westerns would be on the TV things like Seven Brides for Seven Brothers and Oklahoma, another musical. Later on there would be Benny Hill or Morecambe and Wise. The shows that would see you into the new year would have some Scottish dancing and singing and some comedy sketches.

Chapter Three
I want to kill him 1975- 1979

January 1975. Cameron would turn 7 on the 23rd, I'd be 11 on the 27th and Shaila would be 9 on the 31st. There are four days between our birthdays and we are two years apart in age, how's that for timing? Things weren't any better in the house, or our lives. He's still alive unfortunately and we're still suffering. Dad was still asking the same fucking questions over and over, again and Mum was still being beaten up and mentally tortured, and no one was prepared to help. I was still running down to the phone box late at night but I was 2 years older and 2 years bigger and faster now and I managed to beat him two or three times, ring 999 and ask for help before he reached the phone box. But they were still saying that it was domestic and they couldn't intervene. The truth was, it was assault but the authorities let it go on for another 2 years until we got him out of our lives.

Mum started to feel unwell and eventually went to the doctors and they discovered she had a stomach ulcer brought on by stress. She really suffered with it but Dad didn't give a shit, he didn't show her any sympathy, in fact he said she got it because she was worrying about being unfaithful and being found out, so it was her own fault!

I didn't always know what they argued about but it was mainly about the hundreds of affairs Mum apparently managed to have whilst working full time with three kids to look after along with a psychotic, mentally unstable idiot husband.

Sometimes all would be quiet but when he had a drink and an argument would start, usually in bed and the next thing she was getting slapped about. These 'sober attacks' as I called them, didn't happen very often but they did happen out of the blue. For example, one day Dad was in the armchair sleeping and Mum was sleeping on the couch. It was the middle of the afternoon, all was quiet and I was on the other chair watching TV. Dad woke up and looked over at Mum and just got up went over to her and kicked her in the stomach, whilst she was still asleep. This was a shocking thing to see. Mum screamed in pain and held her body in agony. He just walked away!

Everything seemed to be happening in slow motion as I ran to Mum. All I could do was hug her and cry. One thing I did know was that this shit had to stop, but how? That night when I was in bed I couldn't get what I had seen out of my head. I kept asking myself why did he do that to her when she was sleeping, how cruel can someone be to shock someone like that? I was so angry, I wanted to kill him, I wished I could kill him. I thought about how I could kill him.

All sorts went through my head, burn him, poison him, get a big dog to tear him apart, but I didn't have a fire big enough or a big dog either, we only had the poodle and she was terrified of him. The only thing I could come up with was, to stab him when he was sleeping.

I was only 10 or 11 thinking about murder, but I was done with this idiot and the situation we were all in. I didn't care about the consequences as long as he was out of our lives. I didn't think much would happen to me anyway, as I was just a mentally deranged kid who had just had enough.

So I thought about how he was going to die. I needed a knife, a big one and then I realised we didn't have a big knife, we only had the dinner knives and they wouldn't do, I would only have one chance and if I didn't do the job right, God knows what would happen. I had to forget about that plan for the time being. So I couldn't stab him because I had no knife, I couldn't poison him because I had no poison and I couldn't shoot him because I had no fucking gun!

Amid all the turmoil, we were still only kids and we did have our times when we would play and laugh. We played doublers, with 2 tennis balls that we would bounce off the wall or the coal cellar door while we sang a rhyme. Another game we played was called Kerby which was played with a football. For this game, we'd go to the front street and stand on the pavement, one of us on one side of the street and one on the other and we would throw the ball at the opposite kerb and try and get it to bounce back to us. It was a really good game. Sometimes we'd have competitions with the other kids in the street. We liked skipping with a long rope, two of us turning the rope and one skipping. If we were short of a person we would tie one end of the rope to the fence. We were quite resourceful, if something broke we fixed it because in those days you couldn't just chuck things out and get another one, we held onto things.

Shaila and I started gymnastics in the spring of 75, which was something to look forward to. We really liked it. We learnt how to do a front flip and once we learnt to flip that was all we did all summer and we got very good at it. Dad built me a wooden beam to practise on, probably the only kind thing he ever did for me. It helped me practice. I loved the gymnastics. However, after a couple of years, I got fed up and stopped going. I still exercised and did flips until one day I just stopped altogether and then my body started to stiffen up and my muscles started shrinking - the downhill spiral that comes with age.

I often ask questions, like - why did whoever made us create a body that can burn, freeze, break, rip, even be pulled apart so easily? Why don't we have better protection for our organs our skin our brain and what about all the illnesses, diseases, viruses and infections we can get and all that growing old shit that is horrible and painful.

Why can't we stop ageing at 25 years old and stay healthy until one day we just drop down dead, simple! We kids were getting older and started to realise this was our life and as difficult as it was, we were stuck with it. School was difficult at times. It's hard enough for kids to go to school from normal family life never mind kids from domestic war zones, like us. What was in our minds was different to kids that grow up in a kind and loving place.

The home time bell went, I would walk slowly down the road and the nearer I got to the house I would listen out for them arguing, knowing that if they were, it probably wouldn't end well. if it was quiet, that could mean, they'd already had a fight and mum was either beaten up or dead or, rarely, that everything was alright. I used to stand under the back garden window and listen to what was going on in the house, so I could figure out if it was ok to go in, other times when there was violence going on I would just stand and cry for my mum, I was helpless, I could do nothing to help her.

The school started two discos through the week. On the Thursday of every week the five to eight-year-olds from 6.30 to 7.30 and we named it 'Sooties' with an adult in attendance. For the nine to twelve-year-olds it was 7.45 to 8.45 and adults didn't have to stay, and that was called Joe's late night because the DJ was called Joe. Mum would take us to Sooties when she could and it was great to get out of the house for an hour and to be stress-free, dancing and running about. When I turned nine I could go to Joe's late night, if I was allowed. I wasn't at first but Dad had to let me go eventually because I was now too old to go to Sooties. I was allowed to go on condition I didn't speak to any boys. Dad could walk up to the school, at any time to catch me and then I knew I wouldn't be allowed to go anymore.

I had to come straight home as Dad would be timing me and expected to see me back home at 8.50 and not a minute later or he would be on his way up the road for me. I would run straight out after the last record to make sure I was in on time.

I would meet up with my school friends at the disco and we would dance and have a great time. I loved the disco lights. In our assembly hall, we had a big stage and a massive, varnished floor and the DJ was on the stage with his decks. It was really good and felt very grown up.

Our primary school was amazing, even the school meals were great, we got a delicious three-course meal every school day, the cooks were the best and they made tasty soups and roasted whole potatoes that were lovely. Everything that came with the roasties was delicious. The puddings were good too and there were seconds if there was any food left. We were well fed at school, just as well as sometimes we had very little in the house. After going to Joe's a few times I realised I loved to dance, every week I got more confident and tried more moves. The DJ noticed this and over the microphone called me up on the stage to dance. I went on the stage, I had a new kilt on which was blue and green tartan, I loved it and often wore it to the disco.

It was great dancing on the stage and the DJ had all the kids make a circle around me while I danced in the middle. It made me feel great it was the highlight of my week, even if it was just for an hour. But like everything else it was short-lived and there would be consequences, not with him this time but with a bully. Yes, now I had my own bully to contend with on top of everything else! She didn't like it because I was getting some attention at the disco and because I was slim and good-looking and she was fat and ugly. She was about five times my size and that's what she relied on, as bullying cowards do. She also had a couple of pals to back her up.

The bullying started at the disco, I remember it so well. I was about nine and a half, they were the same age, but they were three and I was one. She was trying to bring me down as a show-off and said I couldn't dance. She said everyone was laughing at me, they weren't. This was my first confrontation and it scared me. I had to get away from them because the disco was to finish soon. I thought the best thing to do was to just leave and see what they did.

I walked out and the plan was to start running down the road, if they followed me. Our house was just down a bit of a hill and running down it only took a minute or so, I knew if I got in my gate before they caught me I would be safe, the main bully couldn't run that fast but her sidekicks could. I was right in what I was thinking, I walked out of the school and seconds later they appeared so I ran and made it to my gate and the house - now I was running home for a different reason!

This all started in the summer of primary six. I only had a year until I started high school which filled me with dread as the big bully and one of her sidekicks were going to the same high school. I would have changing schools to look forward to along with the bully and this school was further away, about a mile down the road, all downhill again. Luckily I was quite fit at 12 years old because I had to run up the mile-long road to avoid the bullies, I used to run out of the classroom as soon as the bell went to get a head start.

I would be halfway up the road before any other pupils appeared at the bottom of the hill, home and dry before any of them noticed I wasn't there. I got away with it for ages until they found out how I was managing to avoid them and the urge to bully someone became too much for them.

They started to leave as soon as they could as well, to try and catch me. It wasn't easy to catch me though because I was fitter and smarter and because there were three different ways up from the school, straight up the middle was the easiest way for me but you could go up the right side through a scheme of houses or over to the left side up the side of a woods, far off my normal route, it took much longer to get home but I would take if I had to. Then one day they caught up with me and sprang out at me at the store. I was scared as they pushed me into a corner at the back of the store but they didn't actually do anything it was just threatening words. They let me go eventually and I ran home sobbing. When I got in Mum saw I had been crying, and asked what was wrong. I told her and she said, "I'm going to see the school about letting you out before the other kids."

She and I had a meeting with the headmaster and we told him what was going on and how long it had been going on. He said that under the circumcises it would be best if I got out 10 minutes before the bell. That was the solution, I was to get 10 extra minutes to run up the road away from the people who were making my life a misery. There was no plan to talk to the bullies about their threatening behaviour and how it was affecting me! They were just allowed to get on with it. It didn't stop them terrorising me out of school, from time to time. They kept this up for about 4 years. There came a point when I said I've had enough of this crap. Mum said the only way you're going to get rid of them is to stand up to them, one by one.

She said, "allow them to fight you!" I took her advice when I saw one of the sidekicks coming towards me in a street, on her own.

I had to pluck up a lot of courage to approach her, but I said, "You've been threatening me for 4 years now, so let's settle it. Do you want to fight me?"

"no!" she replied nervously.

I said, "You've been joining in with the bullying for years but now you're on your own you're saying you don't want to fight me or call me names or bully me!"

I was mad because I'd had enough of her and her stupid cowardly pals and my stupid cowardly Dad, making my life a misery. Well for the bullies, at least, this stops now! I told her "Don't come near me again and tell the other two half-wits, to stay away from me as well."

I didn't know how it was all going to pan out but I didn't really care anymore. Luckily the bullying stopped. Now it was only *him* to deal with, but I didn't know how.

It was April and springtime again. I just love spring, it's the most productive time of the year. All the flowers start blooming and baby animals are born. The weather starts to get better and cute little animals come out of hibernation. Everything flourishes and also, my favourite time of year, the summer, is close. We loved the summer because we were off school for 6 weeks, which seemed forever back then. In those days we did get good summers, some years we would have sunshine right through the holidays. It was great because you could plan days out with a picnic and not have to cancel because of the weather. During the summer, the furthest we ever got was the disastrous trip to Blackpool.

Mum would take us to the nearest beach when she could, it took two buses but if we left early we got a decent day out. Sometimes Dad would take us in the car when we could afford to have a car. I think we had two or three different cars over the years, but probably only when they were both working. We would drive about 10 miles to the nicer beach called Gullen Beach, which had dunes and clean clear water, much cleaner than the other beach. It usually had a Mr Whippy ice cream van there, so we looked forward to the little trips we would go on.

Now and again Dad would do these things, but only when he felt like it or he could be bothered, it wasn't really for us.

Growing up in the seventies wasn't easy for us, although others were having a ball, like the hippies - they had a rare old time, between the drugs and the amazing music they made and played. It was a fantastic time to just listen or dance to that joyful music.

Spring passed and we were into summer now. Things weren't any better with the family life, *he* was still an evil bastard. The gambling and drinking had got worse over the years. I was twelve now going on thirteen. I just kept thinking, we need to get rid of this maniac out of our lives and Mum was thinking the same. She started to retaliate against him. If he hit her she hit him over the head with pots and pans, nearly every pan had a dent in it.

If she did retaliate she had to get out of the house quickly, with us, before he had a chance to get hold of her. Those were the times we would go to Grandad's and stay for two or three days or go to Dunfermline to Dory's. One night, he came in drunk and started the usual crap, everyone was in bed. He started arguing with Mum so she got up and headed for the stairs. Dad grabbed a hold of her at the top of the stairs and she was certain he was going to push her down but somehow she managed to push him down in the scuffle. He fell down 8 stairs and lay unconscious. Mum woke us up and told us to get dressed and get our coats and shoes on. Once we were dressed, we reached the top of the stairs and saw him. He lay there, not moving, we didn't know if he was alive or dead but honestly, we didn't care.

It was him that was hurt and helpless this time and I think this was the turning point for Mum. She said, "Just step over him." We did and we were out the door. None of us said anything I think we wanted him to be dead so we could be free, so we just walked out the door, a 13, 11 and 9-year-old walking out the door, possibly leaving their father to die.

We didn't know if he was alright and the saddest part is we didn't care. We went to Dunfermline for a few days, put it all behind us and enjoyed our break, but we had to go back sometime. When we returned Mum told us to wait at the gate whilst she went in to see what was going on in the house. I think she was a bit scared that he'd still be lying there, if he was dead. No one would have found him because no one came to our house. After all, they knew they were not welcome, except for my auntie Margaret who had a brain disorder that affected her mobility, she wobbled when she walked but nothing stopped her, she battled on even though it was crippling her.

She turned up at our door a few times, if *he* was in, my mum had to say she couldn't come in and would make up some excuse. If he was out she would let her in for a cuppa, but a quick one. She was the only one brave enough to come to see my mum and us, I think she knew what was going on and wanted to make sure we were alright. I've got loads of respect for my Auntie Margaret, she was a good person and even though she was suffering she would still be laughing and joking. She was a great woman and my uncle loved her. We waited at the gate as Mum slowly walked down the path and stopped at the door, listening for any noise coming from the house. We watched with great anticipation, we didn't know what she was going to find, but we knew what she could find. Five minutes later she opened the door and beckoned us in, thank God, everything must be alright otherwise she wouldn't let us go in.

Going in the house was strange at first as the last thing we'd seen was him lying unconscious at the bottom of the stairs, but when we went in everything looked normal, there was one thing missing though, and that was - him. We were back and he wasn't in, we didn't know what reaction we were going to get when he showed up, after all we had left him for dead.

Mum said "when he comes in you lot go out to play". She had no sooner said that and the front door opened, it was him, "So you're back."

We kids just went outside, waited nervously and listened. Everything was always down to listening, what we heard would determine what was going on. It was strange as we couldn't hear any shouting or mum crying, just conversation.

He did ask, "Have you got someone else in Dunfermline?" of course she said no, for the millionth time, he shouted us in and asked us if we had seen her with any men when we were there and of course we also said no. But he declared we were all liars and he was going to find out the truth if it was the last thing he did.

Surprised by the fact he did not beat her up, we were confused. Something was changing. I think he became a bit wary of Mum because finally, she had retaliated.

We saw what she was doing and it rubbed off on us. We started retaliating against him too. We were less scared of him now. For instance, when he came home drunk and fell asleep on the couch or the chair we would creep over to the chair under the back window where he hung his jacket and dip his pockets for change. We wouldn't take it all because that would have made him suspicious. It was risky but we didn't care, we were fed up with him telling us to be good when he was always being bad.

One night he came home pissed about 7 in the evening. Mum had made stovies for dinner, which we had already eaten. He came in soaked because it had been raining and proceeded to strip off to his vest and pants, demanding his dinner. Mum brought it through and he started to eat it but after a couple of minutes he started shouting that he didn't have his false teeth in. Mum searched for them but she couldn't find them. He bellowed

" I can't eat without my teeth you bitch!"

"I don't know where they are, they're your teeth *you* should know where they are!" She shouted back.

Mum picked his jacket and trousers up off the floor and chucked them out into the front garden. This was good for us because the change in his pocket would fall out. We'd have to wait a bit to find out if we had any money for the van the next day. Mum threw his shoes at him and one hit him on the head. Mum said "You're moving out!"

"Am I hell." He shouted back and Mum told us to get ready to go to Grandad's. She told him he had better find somewhere to go as she was going to a lawyer to file for a divorce. We went out ahead of Mum and saw coins shining in the wet grass. We collected them and took them with us to buy goodies At that time one of our neighbours' daughters worked in a grocers, that sold sweets. We would go down and if she was working she would give us extra sweets in our pick-and-mix bag, it was great to get almost double the amount.

We would often make fun of Dad when he wasn't in the room. He would hear us but he couldn't see us and he would shout through to us to shut up. We didn't stop, we were just quieter and then our laughter would get loud again and he would storm through, but we would be sitting quietly as though butter wouldn't melt. He didn't know what to do with this, because he knew that we knew he'd heard us, but when he came through we were sitting quietly.

We weren't always making a fool of him, sometimes we played silly games like impersonations of TV stars or people we knew. Cameron hid behind the armchair and put on Mum's wig which was black and wavy, a pair of sunglasses and popped up singing a song that Nana Mouskouri sang. She was a Greek singer with black wavy hair and glasses. It was so funny we would be rolling about laughing until we heard him coming through. Just in the nick of time Cameron would throw the wig back on the dresser and hide the glasses under the cushion, so when Dad reached the living room we were sitting watching the TV. We often had to stop mid-laugh, it was hard to hold it in but we managed it. There were times we'd get away with it and other times we'd either get shouted at or skelped over the head.

Mum took her time about the divorce as all the time, he was trying his best to convince her that it wouldn't be granted because they wouldn't believe what she said and she'd need a witness to confirm her story of abuse. Then one night he came home drunk and started the questioning, I am sure you know what questions by now. Nearly 7 years of the same old, accusations, several beatings, insults, name-calling, mood swings, uncertainty and fear. That was our childhood. Even if things were going well for a few days, you knew it wouldn't last, it was always on your mind, when is he going to turn into Mr Hyde again? That's what I was thinking, most of the time.

We were in bed and I could hear them talking downstairs, not shouting or arguing but actually talking. I heard him saying,

"I think the best thing for us, would be to die."

I couldn't believe he'd said that and I had to hear more, so I got out of bed quietly and put my ear to the floor so I could hear through the floorboards. I heard her say,

"What do you mean?"

"Well" I heard him say, "because you can't tell the truth, it's going to be best that we die, and I've thought of a way to do it too."

I heard Dad open the cupboard, and now he said, "We're going to use electricity."

I was dumbfounded. He was going to electrocute both of them and Mum was agreeing! Why? I couldn't understand but I could not let this happen. Next I heard him saying

"We'll do it naked."

"Ok," mum said.

What the fuck? They're going to electrocute themselves, naked and leave the mess for us to come down to in the morning! I thought. No, you're not doing it. I went to the top of the stairs and sat down so I could hear more clearly, what was going on. I was desperate to discover that I had misheard through the floorboards, but it was true, he was going to kill them.

After I heard that, clear as day, I knew there was no way I was going to let this happen, I ran down the stairs and ran into the living room and there he was standing with wires in his hand! I looked at her and said,

"Why are you doing this ?" I asked, "what about us?"

Mum looked at him and said "She's right, this has to stop!"

Mum took me back to bed, cuddled in and whispered

"It's going to be alright, trust me."

Chapter Four
Goodbye Daddy 1980/1981

Shaila, Cameron and me, all slept in a double bed as there were only two bedrooms in the house. Cameron slept in their room before Dory was chucked out and all the trouble started. I whispered to Mum, "Why did you let him convince you to be electrocuted and naked?

Mum whispered back, "I wasn't going to get electrocuted because I was leaving my slippers on which have rubber soles and they would have saved me but, he would have been dead!"

The next day Mum went down to the solicitors to make an appointment to file for a divorce. She got an appointment two days later and told the solicitor everything. He told her that she had grounds for a divorce. It was harder to get a divorce in those days, you had to have a good reason for it. Personally, I think being assaulted and mentally tormented for seven years was a pretty good reason!

Mum came home that day to find *him* hiding in the cupboard under the stairs because he thought he would catch her with another man in the house. When he realised she was on her own he decided to reveal himself. Mum wasn't surprised and said, "I've filed for a divorce and I want you out of here, soon."

He didn't go quietly or easily, he tried the, "Why should I leave? It's you who has done wrong so you should leave!" but there is no doubt Mum was going to get custody for us.

"I've nowhere to go!" was another tack.

Mum said, "You can go to your mothers, she has a spare room."

That didn't appeal to him because even his own mother couldn't stand him and he knew it. Mum was fighting back, she kept telling him to leave and that she hated the sight of him. They argued and fought for about three weeks, then finally one day, he left and went to the only place he could, his poor old mother's. She would have been about 75 years old and would not have wanted him in her house. Mum felt bad that his mother ended up with him, but she wanted him away from us. Dad went to his mother's and after just a couple of days my gran was begging Mum to take him back but she stuck to her guns for 2 weeks. Finally she gave in feeling sorry for gran and said he could come back on the condition he found somewhere else to live, and soon.

That was bad news for us. We were just getting used to a life without him and it felt great, the house was so much quieter and the fear and dread were gone, for the first time in our short lives the house felt normal. Now he was coming back. Mum promised us it wouldn't be for long but, in the event, it would take another two years to get him out.

During that time, he was more like a lodger to us, a lodger that you didn't want in the house. I think he thought that eventually, somehow, he could talk Mum round. I don't know why he would want to stay, we all hated him and he knew it.

During those two years, we tolerated him, that was all. He had no authority any more although we still had to be careful. During those two years, we got new neighbours who moved in at the bottom of the road. They had a girl and a boy, Cherie and Darren who was about the same age as me and Cherie was Shaila's age.

One day I noticed Darren racing up the road on his bike. He was going fast up and down the street I used to sneak into the front room to watch him rip up the turf on his push bike. He was a bike fanatic, he liked to fix bikes up and go fast on them. We started speaking with them, they were nice kids, brought up properly with a good father who worked hard and treated his wife with respect and kindness. They wanted for nothing, their house was nice inside with nice furniture and they had nice bed sheets and quilts. We had sheets and blankets and in the winter when it was really cold we would have to put our coats on top of us, because we didn't have extra blankets. They had all the mod cons, like an automatic washing machine that spun the clothes as well. We still had the twin tub that you had to put boiling water in the washing side with a hose from the hot tap then once it was washed you took it out and put it into the other side to spin.

Those machines were the best, they were hard work but they really cleaned your clothes and almost rinsed them dry. Darren's family had a big double fridge and a nice big cooker, but the real sickner was that they had a colour TV and we still had black and white. It was great when we were at theirs and we would watch the colour telly.

Eventually we did get a colour TV with a metre in the back that you put money in to switch it on and when the money ran out, it switched off.

Then, one day Darren asked me to be his girlfriend. I hadn't had a boyfriend before due to the fact Dad did not allow me to go near boys, never mind have a boyfriend, but I still said yes. Darren was a nice boy although he really was totally obsessed with bikes.

He would show off, riding up and down the street, doing wheelies and riding with no hands. Darren used to do an Evel Knievel stunt, which involved going down a steep hill at our primary school where at the bottom he had a ramp with some of us lying behind it, so he could jump over our bodies instead of over cars and like Evel did.

It started off with one person that he cleared with no effort. The number went up one by one until there were about six of us lying down behind the ramp. I think the last person got their ass hit so we thought we had better stop before someone ended up badly hurt, it was really good fun though. It annoyed me when he took off with his pals, all on bikes. We didn't have any bikes at that time.

The next Christmas, however, I got a bike and so did some of the other kids in the street, so now there was a gang of us on our bikes. The first place I wanted to go to, was up to 'the camp.' I don't know why it was called the camp, because there wasn't any camp, just a very long hilly road surrounded by fields and countryside. When you reached the top there was a piece of land with a big hole in it, it was quite steep so you'd go down one side and up the other, it was great fun. Of course, Dad didn't know I was going up there, he would have flipped if he knew, but this was retaliation time for us, we were not as scared now to go against him. He had spoken to Darren in the passing a couple of times and said to Mum that he liked him and thought he was a nice boy. We were together for about 2 years, I think Dad had an inkling that I was seeing him but he never said anything about it.

One of the neighbours, who was a single mother, asked me if I wanted a babysitting job on a Saturday night and I jumped at the chance of making some money. It was great, I had a house to myself for a few hours and Darren used to come round the back door and we'd listen to music and have a cuddle and kiss, that was all, we were only about 12 going on 13. At Darren's house, we would sneak into his room and I would just lie on the bed with him and listen to bands called Boston and ELO.

So Mum had to let Dad come back, but no one was happy about it. Obviously, we didn't want the monster back to continue doing his monstrous things, but Mum, being the kind-hearted person she was, even after everything he had done and said, she still let him come back. Mum got a new job as a cook for the kids at a children's home in Edinburgh, in a big old house. It had about 12 bedrooms in it and a big kitchen, dining area and big sitting room. It was set in lovely grounds and was in a nice little town called Morningside. We were allowed to go there from time to time to visit, it was so good there, we loved it. The staff were so kind and good to all the kids and us.

It definitely wasn't one of these homes where the kids were treated badly, everyone was just so kind and considerate, it was a great home.

Time passed, months and then a year and Dad was still there. He wasn't behaving either, he was still terrorising Mum and us for the truth and he was still getting the same answer. Finally he was offered a house and he took it, thank fuck. He had to because the divorce had come through and he had no right to be staying in our home any longer. He packed up his stuff and moved out, halleluiah! thank the fucking Lord! We finally got rid of him. I think that had to be the most wonderful, day of our lives. This was the time we had been looking forward to, all our short lives, it didn't seem real, but it was, it was very real. We were finally free of that controlling idiot, we could do whatever we wanted to now. At first it was strange going to bed with no dramas going on downstairs. Even though he wasn't there anymore our minds were still in that mode, it took a while for that to stop, I suppose we were adrenaline junkies by then, but when it did stop it was great just to be able to go to bed and relax with no fear or anxiety and just go to sleep. He did sometimes still harass us, he would appear at the door saying he wanted to see us. Mum said,

"I'm not going to stop the kids seeing you if they want to."

She asked us if we wanted to see him and we all said no. Why would we after all he had done? Now we had got rid of him, we were all excited to see what would come next. For so long we had been restricted, scared and poor and we knew our lives were going to change now with all the badness out the house. It was like an exorcism and now we could breathe again and learn to live our lives without restrictions and fear.

Now that we could do what we wanted, Mum and I decided we wanted to go to one of the pubs down in the town. It was called the Old Meal Market Inn. It looked good from the outside so we went in to see what we could have for lunch. It was old-fashioned inside with a long wooden bar and wood panelled walls. There were old pictures of the pub when it had been a stop-off for coaches and horses in the 1800's and there was even a ghostly story that goes like this:

The pub was owned by a couple and it is said that the husband went on one of the coaches never to return. The wife was so broken-hearted that she hung herself and now apparently haunted the pub.

The story went that there were times that you could hear banging on the ceiling above, even when there was no one up there. The bouncer there was deaf but he often heard the vibration from above, it was so powerful. One night one of the bartenders' hair was pulled up from the back whilst he pulled a pint and the people standing at the bar saw it happen. Another night when there was a lock-in, the jukebox switched off then suddenly went on and started playing a very old song that wasn't even on the jukebox playlist! That freaked everyone out. One day my brother-in-law went upstairs to check on his son who was sleeping in his pram, and he saw an old lady there with a long black dress and a sad look on her face. At that time he didn't know about the ghost, so he came down the stairs and said do you know there's an old lady up the stairs. Mum said, "Was she dressed in black?"

He replied, "Yes"

"That might have been the ghost you saw!" Mum said.

When he heard that, the blood drained from his face and he looked as white as a ghost himself. I never saw her but I did hear the banging one night and it was loud and scary. But on our first visit, we ordered some lunch and a drink, it was a busy pub and it was the first time I had been in a pub. I'd been *outside* our local pub plenty of times when we took the empty beer bottles down, but never inside. I didn't know what it looked like inside but it smelled terrible, it wasn't a smell that made you want to go in. It was half full of musty old men that would have contributed to the smell. Lunch in this pub was nice and the pub didn't smell bad. Mum went up to the bar for another drink and the bar manager said to her, "You look like the very person we are looking for!"

"What do you mean?" Mum asked.

"I'm looking for a good-looking barmaid and you fit the bill!" he replied.

Mum said, "I've never done bar work before."

"Well I am sure you can learn." He said.

"I've already got a job, but maybe I could do the job part-time?"

"That would be great! You've got the job"

And that was it, the shortest job interview ever.

So now Mum had two jobs and she had more money than she ever did before. She decided to take us on a holiday to Butlins away down in England. We were so excited. To be going on a proper holiday!

The Monster That Lived In Our House

We went by coach from Edinburgh and it took half a day to get there but we didn't care, it was all part of the fun. When we finally got there, the coach pulled into a massive car park with loads of coaches and cars. We checked in and were shown to our chalet. The chalets in those days were pretty basic but we were there and the weather was good and we were ready to enjoy ourselves for a change. This holiday camp was really good, it had some fairground rides, a bar done up like a jungle and best of all, a big disco hall.

There were other eating places and bars that allowed kids in with the adults. We had never imagined it was so good, we went to the fairground on our own, whilst mum sat at a bar, she wasn't a drinker but she had a cider and enjoyed it so that was to be her drink for the next few years.

We even went to the disco by ourselves, it was a big hall and it had all the lights there and of course some drinks and crisps. I think the disco was on most nights and we were there most nights as well. We were only there for a week, Saturday to Saturday. On the Monday I noticed two new faces at the disco, two new boys, good-looking ones as well. They looked alike, I thought they looked like brothers, they were both thin and dark-haired. They had pointy shoes and suits on with white shirts and black ties. They were mods, they danced to The Jam and other mod-type music. They were cool and different, they looked smart and they stood out. I liked one of them better than the other., The one I liked had jet black spiky hair, he was as thin as a stick and had bandy legs but there was something about him, he was really good looking and I thought, he would never look my way, and he never did. Sadly, I was invisible to him, so I just admired him from a distance. I met another boy though, he was called Mark and I just had to settle for second best. Our holiday was almost over, we were leaving the next day. Mum took us to the jungle bar for our last dinner and afterwards we went to the disco, one last time.

I met up with Mark but I watched the other boy most of the night, daydreaming about how great it would be to kiss him. I didn't even know where they came from. The night ended and I said goodbye to Mark and went back to the chalet. Morning came and it was time to go. We all piled on the bus and started the long journey home.

Going into the house with no fear or apprehension was amazing, the monster that lived there was no longer, it was quiet when we walked in, no pressure no fear, all the things we would feel when arriving back to the house of horrors, he was gone and it all went with him, we didn't need to be fearful or worried anymore. As time went on we all became happier and ready to enjoy life for a change.

When we got back, my best friend Lorna came around wanting to know all about the holiday. I told her about the place and then about the two boys and how I fancied one of them. I described them to her and she said they sounded cool. A couple of days later Lorna called me and said, "You'll never know what I've found out,"

I said "what?"

Lorna sounded quite excited. She said John, one of our friends, was talking to her and asked if she knew if I enjoyed my holiday. She had mentioned the guy that I fancied and told him that he and his friend were dressed as mods and that I particularly liked the one with the black spiky hair.

"Wait a minute" he said, "I think I know who they are, it must be them she's talking about", He thought two of his friends that went to St Davids School were away on holiday in Filey and it sounded like them.

He said he was going to speak to them and ask them if they would be interested in meeting Lorna and me. By this time I had long curly hair and big boobs, I was slim and not a bad looking 14-year-old. Lorna was a good-looking girl, she also had something about her that made guys go mad. She also had long curly hair, perms were all the rage at that time, she was slim but had fried eggs for a chest, but she got a lot of attention from the boys, they just loved her.

She couldn't wait to tell me what she had just found out, I couldn't believe it, what were the chances? how could this be?

I had imagined they lived hundreds of miles away and it turns out they lived just down the road, happy days! John let us know that they were going to meet us that night and were going to my house at 7. I needed to get ready quickly, as it was 5.30 already when I got the news. Lorna came up to my house for 6.30 so that gave us half an hour to make any finishing touches and be excited about the fact that I was going to meet the man of my dreams.

We watched out the bedroom window to see them appear at the bottom of the road. It was the same window that Mum had spent all those years looking out of for *him*, but this time I was looking for someone far nicer. The boys appeared and my heart started pounding. We watched them walk up the road and come in the gate, but one of them looked different, one of the brothers I remembered was missing and there was someone tall, skinny and blonde in his place but the one I liked was there!

They knocked on the door and my brother answered and shouted to me, "It's for you sis."

We ran down the stairs and out the door, introduced ourselves, and I found out at last that the boy I had such a crush on was called Martie, Matt for short and his friend was called Murray. He was quite a good-looking guy, I don't think Lorna fancied him much, but I definitely still fancied Matt and I think he liked me too. We hit it off and started seeing each other. I had thought I was in love with Darren, but now I knew I wasn't, because what I felt for Matt was so different.

We fell in love, we were together a lot, we listened to music a lot and danced together at the high school disco and of course, we kissed and cuddled. He was a great kisser and so am I, if I do say so myself. The music we liked then was the Jam, they were his favourite band and we also liked the Beatles the Kinks, Blondie and many others. I started wearing miniskirts and cute kitten heel winkle pickers, black tights and a bomber jacket. We really were the IT couple for a while. Life was great now, it was normal. Matt was about 9 months older than me so he left school before I did and got an apprenticeship in printing, almost right away. His father worked in a factory just down the road and he got him an apprentice position there.

I was officially still at school but I was skipping it most of the time. Now things were changing, Matt was working and making some money and I was in between skipping school and leaving. Christmas was coming again, our second Christmas together. He wanted to buy me a ring, so I chose a ring with my birthstone in it, which is a garnet. I loved that ring and still have it to this day. Of course, things were heating up with us as we were a year older and we wanted to do more than kissing, so I went to the contraceptive clinic in Edinburgh and got started on the pill.

One night, we decided that we were going to do the dirty deed. That night finally came, we jumped into bed and I think we had sex - it was all over in about 2 minutes. I thought, 'I'm sure it's supposed to last longer than that - if that's it, I don't know what all the hype is about!' it seemed pretty shit to me. We were still so young and had nothing to learn from, not like nowadays, with all the porn on line, I'm sure kids know a lot more than we did.

Anyway Matt wasn't a sex fiend so we only did it a few times but we got better at it, I suppose practice makes perfect. We were in our third year and we decided to throw a boxing day party - we had a lot of parties after *he* left. But now I began to realise that there was something wrong with Matt, he was acting weird, I had heard that he had been seen mucking about with a female punk, a few days before. I hoped it was just mucking around and nothing else, but he told me at the party that he wanted to finish with me. It was a bit of a shock I really wasn't expecting it.

I was really hurt and upset, I cried for about 2 weeks. It was like someone had just died. It felt so bad, I was grieving, I didn't know it at the time but that's why I felt so shit, I wasn't going to see someone I loved again and that hurts like hell.

Eventually I started to feel better and got on with things. Lorna got a job in one of the chippies about three miles down the road in the little town Dalkeith. She was there for a few weeks when a vacancy came up for a counter assistant and she asked me if I wanted the job. The owner, Tommy, was a dumpy little guy with a bald head on top and sort of frizzy curly hair running around the rest of his head. He was no looker but he was a very nice guy, he would come at the end of the shift to lock up and take us into town to buy us a baked potato from Spud You Like, which he paid for. Then he took us home. He also had two sisters who worked there, two good looking girls, like me and Lorna. I think he liked to be surrounded by good-looking girls but he was a gentleman and he didn't make any passes at us or advances. He looked after us, he was a good employer.

So now I was boyfriendless but Shaila had met a boy from school called Simon, who was tall and had dark spiky hair.

I didn't know him or his family, although I think Shaila and Simon were definitely in love as they met when they were only 15 and they ended up getting married at the age of 19. They had their firstborn shortly after that. Shaila had a girl and named her Veronica, who, although we did not know it, was going to bring turmoil to the family as she was a pretty horrible kid, sorry to say that V, but it's true. V was selfish and disruptive the kind of kid that would cause a row in an empty house. She would embarrass you, no matter where you were with her. This bad behaviour started from about 1 year old when she started to realise the difference between yes and no and V hated the word no. She became the most challenging thing in our lives, after our battle against the devil himself. You couldn't take her anywhere without a drama, anything from being told she couldn't have something or refusing to move if we were going somewhere and she didn't want to go. She would just refuse to move and we had to lift her out or drag her out even when she got older because she was still acting like a 5-year-old when she was ten.

The start of 1981 wasn't great because I was jobless and had no boyfriend. I still had my friends and Mum though. School was a waste of time for us, as is often the case for kids going through trauma. We didn't have much of an education, we were there, sitting in the classroom but our minds were elsewhere. Kids like us learnt different things like lying, keeping secrets, violence and survival.

Chapter Five
Our Trip To France 1981

My sixteenth birthday was on January 27th, 1981, and now I could go and sign on for benefits. In those days it was easy to sign on, most people thought it was their God-given right to sign on if they weren't working. I signed on and after a couple of months, they got in touch with me about taking a YTS (Youth Training Scheme) position. There was a position at the local Co-op. It paid a little bit more than benefit money so I thought I'd try it and see. I went for the interview, conducted by a small old man with a bald head and glasses who was the manager. I got the position of shelf stacker and general dog's body. There was only one other full-time shop assistant who was also ancient, but she was alright to work with. It was for six months and I learnt how to stack shelves and price the food. I worked hard and did a pretty good job.

I had to go to the store room to get the stock and one day, as I was lifting a box of crisps when the bottom of the box broke and the crisps all fell out. I put them back in the box and taped it up. Then I thought I could be doing with a bag of crisps so I pulled the tape back, pulled a bag out and put the tape back on. This was to become one of the perks of the job. I would open the bottom of a biscuit box and take a packet out, reseal the box and hide the packet under a unit. When I was down there, I would have one of my stolen biscuits or a bag of crisps. No one ever found out, it was my secret.

The YTS finished and of course, there wasn't a job at the end of it so that was me back on benefits again. Happy days, no need to get up early, I could just stay in bed until whenever, great stuff!

Mum now had two jobs, she worked in the children's home and went straight to the pub to do a shift that wouldn't finish until about midnight. She'd do this at least 2 days through the week and she'd be working at the pub at the weekend. She worked so hard for so many years, for us.

Mum decided to go on another holiday, but this time to France. There were flights in those days but not many and it cost an arm and a leg, so she had to find another way to get us over the Channel. The only other way was by coach, rail or hovercraft or a combination. The plan was to go by bus to Edinburgh and catch the coach to London then another coach to Dover where we would catch the hovercraft to Calais, another bus to Paris then a train that would take us to Perpignan.

We were to stay the night there and the next day we would finally reach our destination by train which was a beautiful place called Caney Plache. Of course, it wouldn't go smoothly - nothing ever did in our lives!

We boarded the coach at Edinburgh to go to London. It had comfy seats and a loo. It was going to take most of the night to get there, but we slept most of the way although after about 4 hours the seats didn't feel so comfy. It was about 6 am when we got to London. It was good to get off the bus and get some breakfast. Next was a bus to Dover to catch the hovercraft. It was all so exciting, crossing the channel in an enclosed speedboat. The hovercraft went quite fast and in half an hour we were on the other side. It was great fun.

We landed safely in Calais and then caught another coach to Paris which took 11 hours with a couple of pit stops for half an hour, on the way. It was a long journey and we were all getting tired and grumpy by now. We arrived at the railway station at about 9 pm only to find that the night train to Perpignan had just left! We couldn't go until the morning.

It wasn't great bunking up in a foreign country, especially in a train station in Paris. There was nothing else we could do, it was dark already and we didn't even know how to look for somewhere to stay, we would just have to stay there for a few hours. The night dragged, and dodgy guys were wandering about, Mum branded them as thieves and told us to use our bags as pillows. We drifted in and out of sleep but Mum stayed awake most of the night and cat napped, no one was going to try and steal our stuff. Mum woke whoever was asleep about 6.30. The station was opening up and people were starting to arrive for their trains. Our train wasn't leaving until 9.30 so we had plenty of time to get breakfast. Over the road was a cafe, where we ordered a large cheese omelette to feed five of us and some orange juice and coffee for Mum. The omelette came with a French baguette and butter. The omelette was massive, the biggest omelette I had ever seen, even to this day. We devoured it and were full to bursting. It cost a pretty penny too, a lot more than back home but we enjoyed it and now had a good idea of the prices in France, which it seemed were expensive so Mum was going to have to be careful with the spends.

We caught the train and settled in for another long journey, probably about 5 hours. We were all tired and just wanted to sleep. All us girls were asleep when the refreshment trolley came round. Cameron and Simon, Shaila's' boyfriend, who had come with us, thought it would be a good idea to order a small bottle of beer each. Cameron was only 14 and Simon had just turned 16 but he was tall and looked older so the trolley guy sold them the beers.

The trolley came around quite frequently and they were ordering beers each time because when we woke up about 2 hours later we could hear bottles clinking and giggling going on from where they were sitting and we decided to go and see what they were doing. They already had 6 empty bottles on their table. They weren't drunk, the beers were only small bottles so Mum let them off with it but they were told *no more beer*!

Finally, we arrived at Perpignan. Mum had booked a room in a small hotel that was above a cafe. The man that owned the café, Andre, owned the hotel as well so we had to go into the cafe to see him. He saw us coming or should I say he saw Mum coming and came towards us to greet us. He was a happy French man, very tall and jolly. He took us up to a room with 2 double beds a shower and a sink. The toilet was in the corridor. We were all hungry now, so we went down to the cafe to see what they had. There was some French stuff and chicken and chips that we recognised, so we ordered that to be on the safe side, it was so good and the cafe was nice too. We had a wander around the place, there wasn't much to see, a few shops, an arcade and of course the cafe, which were now all closing up for the night. We went up to the room and relaxed. There was no TV in rooms in those days so we stood on the small balcony of our room and watched the traffic go by. It was crazy, cars were peeping horns all night and we even heard a smash! Perpignan was a different place at night we discovered.

The noise from the traffic seemed to go on all night but got less as the night went on. We woke in the morning to the sun beaming in through the window. We were so excited to get out to explore but Mum made us take a shower first, then we had breakfast at the cafe and then at last, we could go and explore. Mum walked around with us through the shops and into the arcade. Everything looked fine, it was quiet and there was a Pacman and a Phoenix space invaders machine which was fantastic because we loved those games. We had a few games that day while Mum sat in the cafe and had a coffee and maybe a glass of wine. Mum wasn't a drinker but she enjoyed one, now and again.

I can remember thinking 'This is a great day! It's sunny and we were actually in France!' Mum had pulled it off and we only had one more train journey to go and then we would be in another part of France where there was a beautiful beach and the sea, it was one of the best days of our lives.

We went to the cafe for our dinner and ordered chicken and chips again, Mum asked Andre if they had baked beans in France,

With a Gaelic shrug, he said "Not that I know of,"

Mum explained, "They come in a tin in tomato sauce."

He said, "No, I don't think so."

Mum sent one of us up for one of the six tins we had brought with us. We gave it to him to heat up and serve them with our chicken and chips. We told him to taste some. He liked them and said, "I would like to buy some."

We couldn't give him ours because we needed them, so he said he was going to try and import them. We finished our meal and then went over to the arcade to play the Pacman and Phoenix for the last time, it was great fun.

Perpignan was a really good place, with its trees and flowers growing everywhere. It even had a little stream running through it with a nice footbridge. The train was leaving the next day at 10.30 am so we packed our stuff ready and went to bed. In the morning we had breakfast at the café and said our goodbyes and headed to the train station for the last leg of our journey.

It was about 3 in the afternoon when we finally reached the campsite. It was an amazing feeling. We checked in and were escorted to our piece of land to pitch our tent. We started to unravel the tent, that belonged to Darren, my friend from down the street, who had kindly lent it to us. The only thing was it was only a 4 berth and there were five of us. Now it was time to get the poles and put it up, but we couldn't find the poles, we had lost them! No poles no tent, no accommodation to sleep in.

Cameron had an idea to go to one of the shops that sold beach stuff and see if they had anything that would hold the tent up. They had fishing poles with a net on the end, so we thought, if we take the net off we could use the poles which were made of wood to hold the tent up. They might be a bit short but if we could find a couple of bricks to raise the poles, it might just work.

We bought the poles and took them back. This was a nuisance as we were hoping to be down at the beach by now. Now we were going to have to try and put this tent up. We found 4 bricks lying around on the site, so we put 2 on the back and 2 on the front and placed the poles on top of the bricks. It was a perfect fit, we couldn't believe it, once we had it pegged down with the ropes it was perfect as if it had its original poles - job done!

We got changed and headed to the beach, it wasn't far, maybe 100 yards. As we were walking down we could smell the beautiful aromas from the French restaurants and cafes, not that we would be eating French food, but it smelt great. There was also a Wimpy and an ice cream parlour where we would probably eat.

The beach was beautiful, it went for miles and it was so clean, the waves were massive. We just ran into the warm sea and jumped through the waves. They were so big, you got a tickly fluttering in your belly, we still couldn't believe it, us, here in France it was almost surreal. We must have spent 2 hours on the beach, the sun went down, it was starting to get dark so we headed back to the tent and started to blow up our camp beds. We put four of them side by side and one went at the bottom where everyone's feet were but we decided that every night we would swap.

We all slept well that night. We were shattered after all the travelling and jumping the waves. It was already hot when we woke and we were all starving so we got dressed and headed up the street. We found a baker selling fresh croissants. They looked amazing so Mum got five and then we went to the supermarket to get butter and jam and a few other bits and bobs. The croissants tasted as good as they looked and we ate them with peach jam, most mornings.

After breakfast, we went wandering. It was a quaint place with little narrow cobbled streets, about four restaurants, a couple of cafes, a disco, the Wimpy and a juice bar that sold amazing drinks. There was no arcade but there was a harbour and it was beautiful.

The whole place was stunning, untouched because it wasn't really a tourist place yet, so it was quiet on the streets and the beach. The hunger pangs started so we went to the Wimpy for lunch and had beefburgers and a Whippy ice cream and then headed down to the beach to jump some more waves. Simon spent all his time there with a fishing rod, just as well, he was becoming a pain by not helping to clean the tent. After a couple of days, we discovered a lot of ants running about our tent so every day we had to clean it to get rid of them. Simon thought that didn't apply to him. He was a typical lazy selfish asshole of the male kind, which we soon found out was typical of him. Not only did we have ants in our pants and everywhere else, one of the blow-up beds had a puncture, so that meant you'd blow it up and halfway through the night it would be flat, so all of us, except Mum, took turns to sleep on it.

We had been there for a couple of weeks and Mum noticed that the spending money was running dangerously low. No wonder, everything cost a bloody arm and a leg, a coke was about 3 times the price as back home. However there was a restaurant at the beginning of the campsite and Simon and Cameron went in one night to find they were selling frittes, chips as we know them. They ordered 2 portions and the waiter gave them a massive plateful and I think they only cost about 2 francs which was a bit of a surprise, considering everything else was so expensive. The next night we sent them down again with our big frying pan to get chips and sure enough they came back with it full of chips. Mum had a bottle of wine that night and because she wasn't a wine drinker, ended up being sick and a bit hungover in the morning, but we all enjoyed our chips, they were delicious. We still had two days to go before we were due to leave and it was clear that we were not going to have enough money to last us. Mum decided to leave a day early in the hope we could get the coach from Paris to Dover a day early if there were 5 seats available. We left the campsite and caught the train to Perpignan, travelling overnight.

We got to Perpignan, about 7am. We were hungry but we didn't have much money. We had enough francs to buy a couple of baguettes with no filling but we had some butter and jam left, which would have to do.

We went to visit Andre at the café. He was so pleased to see us. He told us that he had something to tell us. He told us he now had some Heinz baked beans and had put them on the menu. He had put a sign on his window saying *Poulet, frittes and baked beans*. He said come in and sit down I have something for you. A few minutes later he came back with sardines in tomato sauce for Mum. He was a gentleman towards her, he had respect for her, something that was never shown to her by the monster.

Mum did not succumb to any of his advances because we were more important to her. We didn't begrudge her the sardines but we were starving. She ate them while we watched. Mum didn't want to be rude and not eat them and she was too proud to ask him for anything for us. We still had the baguettes that we were trying to hold on to for as long as possible but we ate one of them a little while later.

We said goodbye to Andre and headed to the train station to catch the train to Paris. We arrived in Paris at about 1 pm and headed to the bus depot to see if there was any room on the coach to go that night instead of the next day. The girl at the desk said there were only 4 spare seats but we needed 5. So that was that we were staying another night in the train station. We couldn't believe it, not again, please God and this time we were starving and thirsty as well.

We picked a pitch to bunk down on. It was going to be a long night as it was only about 2 pm. We were hungry, thirsty and depressed, all hope gone. We were homeless in Paris, again.

From nowhere a French guy appeared. He was about 5'4, thin and about mid-twenties. He came over to us and asked if we wanted tickets for the tube. We said no but then mum said, "Do you want to buy this tape recorder?" She told him we needed some money to buy food and that we had nowhere to stay the night. He said he would buy it for the price of a room in the hotel over the road and it would be about 30 francs.

We couldn't believe it. He said he didn't have the money on him and would have to go to his apartment for it and he wanted me to go with him. Mum said "no ,"right away, it was an odd request, instead she said we would both go with him. She told the other three to stay where they were until we got back and she said,

"If we're not back in 2 hours, get the police and tell them what's happened."

We left with him, travelled on a tube for a few stops and then got off and then got on another one. We didn't have a clue where we were going and we didn't know this guy from Adam. It suddenly struck us we could be in danger, the second tube journey only lasted about ten minutes and then we got off and started to walk to his apartment. This wasn't good. We started to panic, thinking that there could be a gang of men waiting for us. What the fuck had we done? We'd left three kids at the train station to go to an apartment with a stranger, it just shows you what you're prepared to do when you're starving.

After a walk of about 5 minutes, we got there. He took us up a flight of stairs and then into his apartment. It was ok inside quite tidy and there was no one else there.

He said, "Sit down and I'll get some orange juice and fruit for you," Mum was worried, she whispered "what if he drugs the juice?" he appeared with 2 big glasses of juice with ice and a bowl of fruit, peaches , oranges, grapes and apples.

He said, "Help yourself."

He put the recorder on and that was something else to worry about because it had broken down a few days before. Cameron had fixed it but now we were worried it would break down again. Anyway I took a big drink of juice and started eating a peach.

Mum said, "Are you feeling weird or anything?"

"No," I said, "I feel fine." I told her to eat and drink and she took a drink. A few seconds later she said, "I feel funny"

"No you don't, you just think you do because you've convinced yourself it's drugged."

The recorder was still playing, I remember the tape that was in it was a band from the charts called Chic, a really good disco band. The man turned it off and we started to head back on the 2 tubes. We got back to the train station and were so relieved to see the others.

The man who had introduced himself as Dominic, took us over to the hotel and booked us into a room, but it was only for four people and yes, there were still five of us! He told them one of us was going to stay at his place, I think he meant me - there was no chance, but the guy at the desk accepted that.

We went up to the room, it was a big room with two double beds, but the strange thing was the door into the room opened into the bathroom, so the first thing you saw was a big self-standing bath and the toilet at the side of it and then you went through another door into the bedroom, a strange layout that I've never seen it anywhere else.

Dominic said he would take us to the Champs Elysees. We had not heard of it but we said that would be great. He was a really nice guy, or so it seemed. He said he could get a map down at the train station and he asked me to go with him. Down in the station there was an ice cream stall, he asked, "Would you like an ice cream"

How could I say no? I was drooling already. I got a strawberry one and it tasted amazing. I felt a bit guilty because the others didn't get one, but they got me back in the morning!

He said, "I need to go back to the apartment for more money to buy food and some money for tonight."

Like an idiot, I agreed to go back with him and back we went on the two tubes. When we got to his apartment he locked the door and put the key up on a big wooden keyboard that had lots of other keys hanging on. Now I started to worry, why had he locked the door?

He said, "I'm going to take a shower do you want to have one with me?"

Alarm bells were now ringing loudly and my head seemed to be pulsing in and out, how was this going to pan out?

I was sitting on the couch, stiff as a board, just looking around thinking 'what's going to happen here?' I couldn't think of anything else except him locking the door. The blood was running around my veins at a hundred miles an hour, I knew, if I was feeling like this, there was something badly wrong, and now I knew I was in danger.

I was at the end of my period and had no tampons left and of course, had no money to buy any. I'd had to revert to good old toilet paper. I couldn't believe this was all happening and in a foreign country. I was only sixteen, but I learned a very important thing that day and that was that you should never be fooled if a person is showing kindness to you and assume they are genuine and seem to be a nice person. He showed me that a person can have a Jekyll and Hyde personality. I think we all have elements of that, it's just most of us don't show it.

Dominic came back through with just a towel wrapped around him. He grabbed my hand and said, "Come with me."

We went to the bedroom and that's when everything started to go in slow motion. What was the best thing to do, give in to him or try and fight him off, he was only a wee guy? Then I remembered I had my period. A drama that I had watched a while back came into my head. It was about a guy that was intending to rape a woman in his flat, he had locked the door but as he went to attack her and

she said, "Please stop I have my period."

He stopped and he let her go. Maybe this could work for me.

I said, "Dominic I can't because I've got my period, and it's heavy bleeding, it would make an awful mess."

I could see his brain ticking over and he said, "Yes it would be." He took my hand and said "I've got to get rid of this somehow and he started rubbing my hand up and down his insignificant little piece of pathetic manhood, it didn't take long for him to come all over my hand, it was disgusting and so was he.

I just wanted it to be over and to go back, I started to think about my family and how frantic they would be, not knowing where I was and thinking the worst.

I said to him, "we better go back as my mother will be getting the police because she doesn't know where I am although she knows I'm with you and she knows your name."

That worked because he got ready and we left the apartment. The relief was immense. This guy was mad because he wanted to hold my hand and he gave me one of his earphones so we could both listen to the music from his Walkman. What kind of lunatic was he? He'd held me against my will and was going to force me to have sex with him and now he wanted to act as though nothing had happened. We got back to the train station and

he asked, "Do you want to go to the shop for some food?"

I said, "Yes, let's do that!"

We got to the shop and picked up some bread, butter and bananas and some milk and water. When we got back up to the room Mum was mad.

"Where have you been? I've been going out of my mind!" I told her what happened and she went over to Dominic and said "You better go now or I'll call the police."

Dominic left. Now we worried that he was going to tell the guy at the desk that there were 5 of us in the room. Mum went to the top of the stairwell and listened to see if he said anything but he didn't, he just said goodbye and walked out. Thank God we'd got rid of him and we had some bananas and bread. We had a bath each and went to bed. In the morning I couldn't go for breakfast as I was the fifth person, supposed to be at Dominic's, so I just had a bit of stale bread and banana and some milk whilst they were stuffing their faces with a continental breakfast. I was desperate for a cup of tea, but I couldn't have one. I'll always remember how that felt, when things were so bad that I couldn't even have a cup of tea!

Finally it was time to leave and catch the coach and now we had the problem that there were five of us and we were going to have to pass the desk to reach the front door. What if it was the same guy as yesterday? We decided that if we were challenged, we would make a story up, that I had come back early and there wasn't anybody at the desk so I just went up to the room. We set off down the staircase to the desk, Mum told us to take the luggage outside while she handed the keys in. She did just that, said thank you and walked out. We hurriedly made our way to the bus stop for the coach. It arrived 15 minutes later and we boarded. It was so good to sit there and feel safe.

We were heading home! We got to Calais and caught the hovercraft over to Dover and then caught the coach to London. It was good to be back on British soil again.

When we arrived in London it was late afternoon we were all starving again but we still had no money. Mum said, "We'll go to a bank and see if there's any money in my account,"

"I don't think there is, but there's no harm in looking."

She put her card in the machine and we were praying there might be just a tenner.

There was £30! We couldn't believe it. Mum drew the money out and the first stop was the chemist. The second was a pub to get to the toilet to sort my tampon problem out and while we were there we had a half cider each, it was cold and fruity and it was so good. We drank up and then headed to the chippy for fish and chips and cans of coke for us all. When we got back to them, they couldn't believe it, we had food and drink with us. It was a feast and it was amazing to finally get something substantial to eat after about 3 days of not very much at all. We caught the couch to Edinburgh and got home in the early morning. It was such a relief to get back into the house. One thing was for sure, we wouldn't ever forget our trip to France! We didn't know it at the time, but the holiday to France was to be the first disaster of many more to come.

Chapter Six
Build a new life 1981/83

We got back from France in one piece, God knows how. We didn't know it at the time, but the holiday to France was to be the first disaster of many more to come. I thought it was about time to build a new life, I wasn't quite sure how because I had no money except social money, which only barely keeps you fed. Mum had her two jobs still, so it could be worse, but I wanted to have my own money and independence. It wasn't going to be easy with no school grades or experience other than the 6 months in the Co-op.

A couple of months went by and I still had no job or money. It was September now. Out of the blue, I got a phone call from my sister Dory saying that the whisky bond she worked in was looking for temps to help with Christmas orders. She arranged an interview for me. I had to go to Dunfermline for the interview, so I went the night before and stayed with Dory. It was nerve-wracking as it was only my second interview. I really wanted the job and to get off benefits, it would also help my financial and mental situation. I could feel myself slipping into depression.

I went to the interview and I felt it went well. They phoned the next day to say I had the job. Happy days! Things were looking up at last. I started the first week in November until 23rd December. It was going to be a good Christmas. It was hard work and hard to keep up with the conveyor belts with the bottles on. The first step was in the bottling area at the back. It had about six lines that all started there. At the beginning of each line, there was a big metal disc that went round and round, that's all it did, there were boxes of 12 empty bottles on a pallet and you had to put the bottles on to the plate by turning each box upside down and placing the bottles onto the moving plate without the bottles falling. Then they would just go round with the plate and slip onto the moving belt that carried them through to the bottling area where they got washed and then filled with whisky, labelled and then packed. Before they got packed you had to sit on a very high stool at the belt. There was a wooden box with a horizontal light inside. At the front it was cut into the shape of an upside-down bottle. You had to catch the bottles before they reached the box and turn them upside down with one hand and place them in the box. The light shone through the bottles and you were responsible for finding anything trace of dirt or glass in the filled bottles or spotting if the whisky was cloudy. This was called sighting.

Every bottle had to be clean and clear of any debris, the only thing you should see in a bottle of liquor is bubbles rising to the top, so you lifted the bottle off the belt with the right hand, laid it on the box for a second or two whilst you were looking at it and then lifted it off with the left hand and placed it on the belt to pass through the labelling machine and then on to the packing, also done by our fair hands.

It was hard to do at first as you needed to have some speed or the bottles would gather too quickly and fall off the belt, holding production up and impacting everybody's bonus. Each shift had a rotation of staff. Everybody would be in the bottling hall at some point for about 2 hours and the same went for the sighting and packing. Packing wasn't so hard. The bottling hall was the hardest physically. The boxes were not that heavy as they only had 12 empty glass bottles in them, it was getting them on the metal disk quickly enough to avoid a build-up of bottles. It wasn't so bad lifting them from the top, then the middle, but when you reached the bottom that's when you started to slow down, the pain in your back slowed you down on top of feeling dizzy because you are constantly turning around to pick them up, then bending down low for the bottom ones - up and down and round and round, it's making me dizzy just thinking about it! As time went on you got used to it and the bottling hall became easier. I still had a sore back at the end of the day and a sore neck, but at least I was able to catch up with the line with time to spare. I got so good at it that I had spare time when the disk was full of bottles, I couldn't fit any more on. I would sit on the boxes until there was space on the disk for more, it was the same with the sighting box, I got so quick that eventually I was waiting for the bottles to come down the line. I worked there for the three months, it was a good laugh, with Dory and her pals Lorna and Bev. We were in stitches nearly every day, laughing. We worked for Bells Whisky and it was a great job. The bus there and back was free, all our meals were free, we got a good bonus every week if our line ran well and everybody worked hard. I doubt you'd find a company these days to give all that away. It's just blood, sweat and tears now for very little money and that's the way employers want to keep it. Why don't all you greedy bastards who treat their staff like shit and pay shit money take a leaf out of Bells Whisky's book to get the best out of your staff? At the very least treat us like human beings, not robots or something you've just stepped in.

Bells made sure the staff got to work whether they had money or not, they also made sure they were fed. They always put on a big plush Christmas party and you got a bottle of whisky for the New Year, not that I drank whisky but my new brother-in-law liked it, a bit too much it turned out.

Dory's marriage to Raymond didn't last long. They both smoked weed for a while, but Dory wasn't really into it, she was more interested in concentrating on her job and keeping her life on an even keel. After all that happened to her, she'd had enough drama. After the trip to France, we went to their house for Christmas and New Year. ,It was a white Christmas as it snowed for days leading up to the day. We had a great time, I remember playing the game *Frustration.* They had a few bottles of spirits, sparkling in the lights of the Christmas tree. There was Cointreau a beautiful-smelling liquor, when the bottle was opened you could smell orange. I had a sip. I didn't like the taste much but it smelt amazing.

Summer of 1983 was around the corner and Shaila and I decided to go to visit Dory for a few days. I asked my friend Lorna if she wanted to come, and she said yes, so off we went on the two-bus trek. We went from Friday to Monday as Dory and her partner were working. There wasn't much to do there unless you went into town. At 16 we were still too young to drink. Raymond wasn't much of a drinker, he and my sister were still hippies, he had long blonde hair, was tall and slim and sang in a band for a while. He was quite good, I recall. He introduced me to Pink Floyd's Dark side of the Moon and when I heard The great gig in the sky I just wanted to die and go to heaven because if that's what heaven sounded like, it must be amazing. Another thing Raymond introduced me to was weed. We noticed he was smoking and that it was not tobacco. It smelt strong and I asked him what it was. He told us it was cannabis, a plant you can smoke and it makes you feel good.

"Oh really," I said, "in what way does it make you feel good? He said, "It makes you feel happy and chilled, do you want to try it and see for yourself."

Lorna and I looked at each other and nodded,

"Yes we'll give it a go."

Raymond passed us this thing that was smoking away on its own, he and Lorna took a drag and then I did too. Lorna seemed to be alright and had a big smile on her face. I think a minute passed before I felt a really heavy feeling pushing my head down. It felt like a ton of coal was pushing my neck and head down, it was horrible. Then I started to feel sick so I ran to the kitchen sink and threw up, repeatedly. Every time I lifted my head up I had to lean on the sink and there I stayed for about an hour before I could eventually move to go up the stairs to bed, to sleep it off.

Morning came and as I came to, I could see Lorna was talking to me although she was talking funny, her lips seemed to be sticking together. She told me that she and Raymond had been to get cigarettes and when they were driving by the shore, she had seen an ice cream van in the middle of the sea.

"I don't think an ice cream van would be in the sea, Lorna" I scoffed but Lorna swore blind so I gave up and just said "Ok, then, it must have been."

That was my first encounter with any drugs, it wasn't a good introduction, but unfortunately, it didn't put me off.

Another winter was creeping up on us. I was hoping the whisky bond was going to take me on again and soon after I got word from Dory saying I had been chosen to go back again. Happy days! I was going to start making some money again.

We had a good Christmas and New Year, that year with one of our infamous New Year parties. We'd had a few parties over the years, much to the annoyance of our neighbours - *The Monster* hated them and they hated him, he feuded with them for years.

It had all started when he fought with Jim next door because he thought he fancied Mum, I think that there might be some truth in that because Jim's wife was an ugly, fat troll.

So for years this went on. We weren't allowed to play with their kids either, but when our parents and theirs were out at the same time, we would go sneak through to their house for a while.

Jim's wife was mad and one night for some reason she played the song Enola Gay over and over again, so loud, it got on our nerves, so we wrote a note-

This is Mrs Archibald from down the road, could you please stop playing Enola Gay as I'm getting sick of hearing it.

We posted it through her door. The next thing we saw her run down the road to Mrs Archibald's, then a few minutes later she came running back up and started shouting through the wall between our houses and whacking it with a stick, I think she realised it was us. We would do silly stuff like that to get a laugh.

My next birthday was my 18th on January 27th, 1983. I was still single after Matt bailed on me so I thought it was about time I found someone else. Mum and I started going out. She had her job in the pub, which helped me to meet people. There used to be a good crowd in and the local biker chapter, the Barbarians, started drinking there. They were good customers, most of the guys in the chapter were polite and a good laugh, they didn't want trouble and they didn't cause any, not in the pub anyway. They were a good deterrent for trouble. People knew where they stood with them, they were good bodyguards as well.

One night I was out with a friend Jules whom I had met at school. One morning at school the classroom door had opened and there was the headmaster with a girl called Julie We were in primary five when she joined the class. She had thick ginger hair and ginger skin to match, she wasn't pretty, her skin was rough and she had misshapen lips. I felt sorry for her, everybody was staring at her. The headmaster said, "This is Jules she's joining the class today, make her feel welcome,"

I thought good luck with that one, because being ginger, she was a target right away.

It must have been daunting for her with everybody staring at her. She sat down, the lesson started then it was morning break. Usually, we had break time outside whether we wanted to or not, except in very bad weather. I never gave Jules a second thought as I ran out the door with the other classmates. When we got back in Jules was just sitting quietly with her head down, probably trying to be invisible. Next was lunch time and she sat by herself during lunch. I felt sorry for her she looked so sad and lonely. I was going to Grandads that day after school and I noticed Jules was walking in the same direction, so I decided to talk to her.

I asked her where she lived and she said a street just over the road from my Grandads. We walked together she seemed nice. I said I would come and meet her in the morning and walk to school with her. I saw her face light up with relief.

"I'll see you tomorrow here at 8.45." I said.

The next day she was waiting at the end of the street for me and we walked up to the school and went into class together. I could feel her relief. I had never really had a best friend so we stuck together that day and every other day from then on and became best friends until high school.

Her childhood hadn't been very good either, they'd had to escape a violent father. They were English and they came up to Scotland to live. They were put in a block of flats that weren't the best of housing but I suppose was better than the circumstances they had been in. We got on really well, Jules loved to dance and so did I, and she had suffered domestic abuse as well. I never met the father but her mother was a small woman with a big voice. She came across as quite an angry loud person, I think Jules was a bit scared and wary of her.

Chapter Seven
Stealing, Fighting and Turning 18 1985

I was the only one who made any attempt to be friends with Julie and we became best friends for a couple of years. She loved to dance, and so did I. We used to put the music on and just dance around a room until we were knackered.

Her family was probably as poor as we were. There was her, her sister, and three brothers. They had problems, they'd come from England up to Scotland, fleeing from an abusive father. Her mother was like our mum, a hardy wee woman, although she wasn't the best mum in the world to Jules. She was quite an angry person who did a lot of shouting and would lash out as well. She was mainly all mouth and Jules spent a lot of time at our house for those reasons. The Monster was still there at that time, but it was during the retaliation period when he was losing control. Jules and I hung about in the bedroom if he was in or in the living room when he was out or took ourselves out and about.

One day, we decided to go to town, and we took Shaila with us because she was being a pain. We didn't have much money, just enough for bus fares and something to eat. It's not great going to shops with no money, so we decided to try and nick something. I think the first thing we decided to steal was the Fleetwood Mac single track called "Tusk." It was in the charts at the time and we loved it. The idea was to go into a shop with our jackets on our arms then use the other arm to pick up records, look at them, then slip one under our jackets and walk out. Shaila had to wait outside as she was too young for shoplifting. She wasn't happy, so I promised her we would get her something as well. We put the plan into action, and it worked. We got out of the shop with two "Tusk" records, we couldn't believe it.

Stealing the records had been so easy, it spurred us on to steal more. We got some sweets, a poster each and two or three other things. We stole two of each thing. It was about 3 in the afternoon and we thought we should call it a day, but we'd forgotten about getting something for Shaila. We left our haul with her and went into the shop, John Lewis. I'd asked Shaila if she would like earrings and she said she would. Jules and I went in and I picked up a pair of studs to look at, then instead of putting them back, I kept them in my hand, and we walked out of the shop. But this time, we were seen. The security was on our tail, and we felt the hand on our shoulder—they had caught us!

We were marched up to the office, and they phoned the police. The police arrived about ten minutes later and searched us for more contraband but found nothing because it was all in the bags that Shaila had. I had just remembered she was still waiting for us. I knew she'd be getting worried and she had no bus fare to go home on her own. I knew I had to tell them she was there. One of them went down and brought her up with the bags. Of course, they looked in the bags and they found two of everything. The police asked Jules what belonged to her and she pointed out one of everything.

They told her to take her stuff and go home. It didn't make sense, as it was obvious what we had done, stolen two of everything. They even asked us who nicked what, and I told them it was me who nicked everything. I did that because I knew Jules would end up in serious strife if her mother found out she had been arrested for shoplifting. Even though the Monster was still in my house, I didn't care. I still took the blame. Those bloody earrings—we would have been home and dry if we had just gone home. They let Jules and Shaila go home, and they took me down to the police station, put me in a cell, and phoned Mum to come and get me.

I waited in the cell for ages as she had to get the bus in. I had time to think about how disappointed she would be in me. I didn't like being a criminal who'd got caught, so I thought it'd be best to give up my criminal career, now. When I saw Mum, I just burst into tears. I saw the disappointment in her eyes. I had brought more trouble to her and that made me feel bad. When I got in, I just went up to my room. The police had said that they would be filing a report to the children's panel, and we would be hearing from them to attend a meeting.

When Dad heard what had happened, he came up the stairs and used the information as a weapon against me. He said; "What the hell did you think you were doing shoplifting?" I didn't reply, and he said, "You'll end up in a home for this because you're too young to go to jail. They'll take you away, and you won't see any of us again!"

He was enjoying implanting even more worry and despair in me as if the last seven years weren't enough.

I didn't give a fuck about ever seeing his ugly face again, but my Mum and my brother and sisters—I couldn't bear that.

It took a few weeks for the panel hearing to come up and he made sure I suffered every day with the idea that I would be sent away. I was worried and scared. I did regret it and I was going to tell the panel that I had learned my lesson and wasn't going to steal again. I hoped they would let me off. So that's what I did, and that's what they did! They saw I was sorry and let me off with a warning. I was so happy to be free, but I knew that Dad wouldn't be pleased when he heard this news. When we got in, he asked what happened, and Mum told him. He just looked at me and shook his head in disapproval. He was disappointed that his daughter hadn't been locked away! How horrible is that? That's why he was called the Monster—because he was vile and horrible.

Back to the night out with Jules and her friend Avril, who was a bit scrawny, but nice enough. We started the night off in the Old Meal. Mum was on that night as it was a Saturday night. We had a few drinks and then headed over to a place called the High Spots for a few and a dance. When we got there, Avril's boyfriend was there sitting with four girls. I knew who he was, he was an arsehole, sitting flirting with one of the girls. Avril was getting mad, and Jules said, "If I were you, I would go over there and give her a slap."

The girl was big and ugly, so despite the little bird that she herself was, Avril did just that. She went over, slapped her fat face, and then walked out. We followed and started to walk up the road. Avril's boyfriend came out and caught up with her. The girl came out too, raging, shouting, and following us up the road. Of course, she was angry—she had just been slapped! Jules shouted at her, "Shut up, you stupid cow!"

Well, that just added fuel to the fire, and she started running after us. By this time, Avril, Jules, and the arsehole that caused all of this had disappeared around the corner!

So I was the one she got hold of, and as I said, she was big and ugly. She punched me a couple of times, so I grabbed her face with my nails and dug them in. She pushed me away and I landed on the road. Next, she grabbed my hair, so I put my foot between her legs and pushed. The more she pulled, the more I pushed. Her friends stood and watched. Thankfully, they didn't join in. She let go of my hair, and I removed my foot.

She said, "Tell your friend I'll be seeing her!" and walked away.

I realised in that moment that in fact, Avril was not even my friend, Jules was and where was she? They were nowhere to be seen! I staggered over to the Old Meal. Mum saw the state I was in and took me upstairs and wiped my face and hands. I stayed up there until the pub was closed and then we went home. I didn't go out the next weekend because my face was still a bit bruised, but we were out the next week again and went to the High Spots, hoping the girls weren't there.

They weren't there at first, but they appeared later on. I must admit I was a bit scared because I didn't want to fight again. It was only me and Jules. I had an idea. I phoned Mum at the pub and asked her to get some of the bikers to come along to escort us back to the pub. Five minutes later they were there outside, waiting. Four big guys, with long hair, leathers and big boots. We left the bar and walked back with them. It was like walking with giants, so needless to say, the girls didn't follow and we got back safely.

I was working in the bar by this time, and a couple of weeks later, I was working on a Saturday night when my opponent walked in with a couple of friends. She came up to the bar. I didn't know what was going to happen, but she just ordered drinks and I served them. To my relief, nothing was said. I didn't want any more aggro, and it looked like she didn't either.

I didn't work in the bar for long, maybe about six months. I didn't like it much, serving drunks and listening to their problems. I didn't give a flying toss about them. You would get the rude arseholes and the ones that live under a dark cloud. You get them all in a pub. I just wanted them all to piss off. They didn't, so I left. I was also scared I might encounter the ghost when I was there by myself. That would really freak me out, and I knew I'd run out the door and never return, so I thought I would leave instead.

I had a new job to go to after a week off. It was in a whisky bond about five miles up the road, which also put on a bus for the staff, but it wasn't free, nor were our meals. The wages were quite good for my age, however. I had just turned 18, so I was quite happy to go back into it.

Turning 18 wasn't a big deal for me, maybe I was just grateful I was still here! Going out and drinking legally was the only difference because we had been going out long before and probably started drinking around 15. We would get a can of super strength lager, one between two. We didn't get drunk, but we got tipsy. The amounts got bigger every year. When we were about sixteen, we moved on to a can each, sometimes one and a half.

I remember when Dad came back to the house. He didn't have any authority over us anymore, he was basically a lodger but was still mentally deranged. It was only due to Mum being the kind person she was and the fact that his own mother begged Mum to take Dad back, again always thinking of someone else. She had said he could come back under the condition that he was a lodger until he got somewhere else to live.

Mum started fighting back. Dad was still accusing her of the same stuff, and she was still giving the same reply. The attacks were not as often, but when they did come, Mum would pick up pots and whack him with them, over the head mostly. I saw this happen three or four times. She didn't care anymore; she'd really had enough. He had a long, thick stick with a head on it, a branch from a tree. It was like a big club, the kind you would imagine a man from the Stone Age would carry. Dad kept it in the cupboard in the kitchen. He said it was for protection against burglars, but Mum thought it was for her. One hit from that and she'd be dead, so once she picked the club up and struck out. It missed him, but I think he was stunned and then realised that she meant business. Mum had nothing to lose, we were older, and she had already told her solicitor everything, for the divorce. The police had it on record too. Dad may have been mentally deranged, but he wasn't stupid. He knew the odds were stacked against him. If she did kill him in self-defence, she'd probably get off with it. Mum got rid of the club the next day, just in case either of them picked it up again. Eventually, he moved out, and we washed our hands of him. None of us wanted to see him again, ever.

I had been working in the whisky bond for a few weeks and I'd got myself new clothes, shoes and a red biker jacket. Things were looking up. I could go out at the weekend with my new gear on. One Saturday night, Mum and I decided to go out to a charity night in one of the pubs down the road from where she worked. If it was rubbish, we could always just go up to the Old Meal for a few.

When we got to the charity do, it wasn't so busy. There was a DJ there with his decks and he was playing some good music. More people arrived, and it got busier. It looked like it was going to be a good night. Halfway into the evening, a gang of lads came in, about five of them. They were a bit loud and rowdy, but they were quite funny. The charity night was going well with its raffles and guess how many sweets are in the jar and so on. They were collecting a lot of money.

We were enjoying ourselves, and everybody was having a great time. One of the rowdy guys came up to me and asked if I would like to dance. I always said yes if a man asked me to dance because I thought it rude not to. He was tall, a bit podgy around the waistline, his hair was thinning on the top, and the colour was a combination of strawberry blonde and ginger. He also had a ginger moustache. He said his name was Harry. He wasn't really my type, but he made me laugh. We had a few dances and a little kiss at the end when the slow record came on. He was a good kisser. I think if someone is a good kisser, it's a great start. If I kiss someone who slobbers all over my face, I start thinking they might not be much good at other things - if you know what I mean! So this fellow had the kissing going for him but not much else. I didn't consider him a good-looking guy, but he was really funny, so when he asked me out on a date, I said yes, although I didn't fancy him. A few dates later we became a couple. He was kind and generous, but I was not in love with him.

I knew that he was falling for me, and I thought I should really end it with him because I didn't feel the same, but I didn't want to hurt him. We had been together for a couple of months but hadn't slept together yet. It was coming up to Christmas, and he was coming around to finish a drawing of a ballerina he was painting on my wall. He was an artist, he drew superheroes mostly from Marvel comics, but he could draw other things too, so I said I wanted a black wall with the outline of a ballerina, done in white. I was expecting him about 7 o'clock. We had been given a half bottle of vodka from the whisky bond for Christmas, so I decided to pour myself a vodka and lemonade. It was only 5:30.

I put on ZZ Top. They were my favourite band at the time. I enjoyed the drink, so I had another one, and then another. By this time, I was blaring out the music and half-pissed. It was almost 7, and he was due to arrive at any minute. ZZ Top and the vodka were making me randy, and I felt like jumping on him when he arrived. The door bell went, and Mum shouted, "It's for you."

"Send him up," I shouted down.

Harry came into my room and said, "Are you pissed?"

I answered, "Maybe a bit!"

I poured him a drink and myself another. I said, "Do you know what night this is?"

He said, "Nope?"

I said, "It's your lucky night, mate," and kissed him passionately.

He asked, "Are you sure?" and I replied, "Hell yeah, let's do this."

We ripped each other's clothes off and had a great first bonk. He knew what he was doing, as he was about 7 years older than me. He was the first for me after Matt. Now we had slept together; the relationship was sealed. I wasn't going to pack him in.

We were probably together for about eight months when one night, after a great time out in town, I realised I had to tell him that I loved him. He was over the moon, as he had told me he loved me before, but I had never said it back until then. Now, I genuinely felt it.

Our relationship was going great. We would go swimming together and of course, enjoyed our boozy weekends. He had a big family, with four brothers and a sister. One of his brothers was short, a bit dumpy, with a bald head rimmed with hair and he was very funny. His wife was small and skinny, with a glass eye and wiry hair and she had a heart of gold. We often visited them throughout the year, usually for parties, New Year and Christmas. Their house was the centre for family gatherings.

One New Year, we played truth or dare. I chose a dare, which was to take my dress off and run around the block in my underwear. I accepted. They thought I wouldn't be up for it, but I had a petticoat on under my dress. To their disbelief, I whipped my dress off, ran outside in the icy cold and had a great time running around the block with the kids.

A couple of months after I told Harry I loved him, I noticed a change in his attitude. It was like he now had a hold on me. He started accusing me of being unfaithful. One day, after work, I was exhausted and went to bed for a couple of hours before dinner. I sleep nude, and Harry knew this as we both slept naked. That day he came into the room and accused me of having someone else in there. I was taken aback as he had never behaved like this before. I defended myself and pointed out that my mother was downstairs, making it even more absurd. I didn't like the way our relationship was going. He was angry and sometimes made me feel terrible. Our relationship was no longer the same. I didn't understand why he had become paranoid and suspicious when I had just fallen in love with him and wanted to be with him, no one else. Shades of the monster was rearing its ugly head.

During our two years together, he attacked a couple of my old school friends, Murray and his brother Des, over nothing. One night, after we had been out separately with our friends, he arrived home before me. When I arrived five minutes later, he accused me of having an affair. I told him to stop the nonsense, but he pushed me and I landed on the bed. I got up, headed towards the door and said, "I'm going to find someone else and leave you one day!" And soon afterwards, that's exactly what I did.

A couple of weeks later, Mum and I went to the Old Meal on a Sunday night for a jamming session. Musicians and singers joined together to play songs for fun. When we arrived, there were a couple of guys with guitars and a good-looking guy with a microphone introduced himself as Bradley, or Brad for short. He started singing a blues song called "The Hoochy Coochy Man." He had an amazing voice and played the harmonica brilliantly. He was tall, maybe about 5'10", with a long torso and short legs, slim and had a cute arse.

I asked Mum about him, and she said he was married with a young son. My brother Cameron, however, thought Brad and his wife had split up, which was music to my ears. Every Sunday, I watched him, quickly falling under his spell. He was amazing, but I felt invisible to him.

The Sunday jamming nights were popular, and eventually, the jammers formed a blues band called Stealing the Blues. They found a drummer, who was amazing despite his looks. A few weeks passed and I was getting nowhere with Brad. Everyone knew I fancied him and Frank, the bass player told him how I felt. Brad asked me bluntly

"Do you want to fuck?"

"Yes! I do!" I replied. and I said yes.

We went to his place and had a great time.

In the morning, he said

'I feel like shit!"

"Thanks!" I said.

"Nah, it's not you, it's the drink." He told me.

We got dressed the rest of the band arrived. They didn't seem to be surprised to see me coming out with Brad and gave me a lift to the bus stop. Brad and I kissed goodbye. We didn't mention meeting again, but I knew I would see him on Thursday. The pub had booked them to play again, so I knew I would see him, whether he wanted to or not.

Thursday arrived, and Harry went to his usual snooker tournament. I told him I was going for drinks with Mum, which was true. At the pub, Brad and the band played. During their break, Brad didn't come over to talk to me, and I felt invisible again. After their last song, I said to mum

"Mum, that's it, if he doesn't come over in the next five minutes, I'm out of here!"

Five minutes passed and I felt like it had just been a one-night stand. It was embarrassing. I was going.

As we walked out, I heard my name.

"Hey, we're going to the Greyhound, you coming?"

I nodded happily..

At the Greyhound, Brad told me he was splitting from his wife. I told him it didn't bother me. He said he liked me and asked if I wanted to go home with him again. I agreed. This time, we weren't as drunk, and we had a great time. In the morning, he asked me,

"Well, what do you think?"

What do I think about what?" I replied

"What do you think about us becoming a couple?"

"Yeah" I said, "I like that idea!"

Chapter Eight
The man of my dreams 1985/1990

This was amazing! I'd finally got him, he was mine, I thought I was going to burst with excitement.

I had spent two nights with Brad, the first night I'd simply told Harry that I went to Mum's, as she'd had too much to drink and I was worried about her. He bought that, but I didn't know what to tell him the second time. I just decided that Harry and I were done so I didn't say anything I just didn't go back to the B&B we had been staying in. A few days went by and Harry was phoning every day. Mum was having to tell him I wasn't in, which I wasn't, most of the time, because I was with Brad.

Before I started seeing Brad, Harry and I were supposed to be moving up the road to another B&B and that just happened to be next door to the B&B Brad was moving into and the one I was moving into with him! What a shambles, what was I going to do?

First of all I needed to tell Harry that we were finished and that I wouldn't be moving in with him. I didn't tell him that I was moving in next door with Brad. I didn't want to hurt him by revealing all that, he was already terribly upset, crying, begging me to stay, promising he would change. I just told him I had fallen out of love with him and couldn't be with him anymore. It was horrible, I really felt bad, but when I was in Brad's arms I was so happy, I felt secure and safe. He was the type of guy that would stick up for you and your family, he wouldn't see any wrong done to us, he wasn't afraid of anyone or anything. He was brave but sometimes too brave. As time went on, I noticed he was very politically minded, I knew nothing about politics and not much more about religion but he'd studied religions and had his opinions about that too. He was optimistic and positive, he didn't like negativity, he always said "there's no point in being negative". The thing was, he couldn't have picked a more negative or pessimistic person to be with, than me!

We were definitely chalk and cheese in that respect, he was nine years older than me, so he had grown up in the rock and hippy era, but he liked a wide spectrum of music. He had Pink Floyds, Dark Side of the Moon. I knew who they were and I loved that album. His music collection was massive. He put on a band called Led Zeppelin, whom I had never heard before, and I didn't like what I was hearing. The singer, Robert Plant, just screeched and screamed. Brad couldn't understand why I didn't like them. A few years later, when I was a bit older and still with Brad, he introduced me to a lot of great music, rock, blues, and Cajun. I ended up loving Robert Plant's voice, he is a rock god. Brad could sing, but he couldn't dance. I refused to dance with him because he was so embarrassing.

So, I had left Harry for Brad. Harry moved into the new B&B, and we moved in next door to him. Honestly, you couldn't make it up. It wasn't easy trying to keep it a secret. He eventually found out that I was seeing Brad, but I don't think he ever knew that I was actually living next door to him.

Brad and I were having a great time, drinking every night and enjoying amazing sex sessions. He also smoked cannabis and reintroduced me to it, though I wasn't sure about it after a disastrous experience last time. He reassured me, suggesting I take a small draw at first, to see how it felt. Reluctantly, I took the joint from him and drew gently - it was okay. This time, the weight of the world wasn't on my shoulders, instead, I felt light-headed and surprisingly good. Unlike the last time, this experience was enjoyable. I took a few more draws and soon found myself high as a kite. Unfortunately, from then on, I was hooked and became a long-term smoker.

We began to paint the town red, getting drunk and stoned nearly every night. The band played every Thursday and Sunday, and the band were getting gigs in different pubs in various areas. It was a fantastic time—sex, drugs, and rock and roll.

I lost my job at the whiskey bond not long after we met because the factory closed down. So here I was again, jobless. Brad wasn't working either, he had been employed at the pit but was on sick leave due to the stress of his divorce and the battle to keep seeing his son.

He loved his son Kendal and was determined to fight for him. It wasn't going to be easy, as he didn't have a permanent place to stay. We were at the B&B, but we only had a single room and shared the kitchen and sitting room. There were three other residents there. One was an older man named Pat, a barber who cut hair in his local pub on Saturdays to make drink money. He was on social assistance, as we all were, and no one cared. Anyone on social assistance needs extra money, who can blame them? It's all very well for people sitting with loads of money saying, "Get a job," or "You should have done better at school then you could be a lawyer or a doctor."

Firstly, not everyone on this planet can be a high-end worker. There aren't enough jobs for everyone. Secondly, not all kids have the capability to become high-end workers. Many of us can only take in a small amount of education because of the trauma we are going through.

Whose fault was that? Not ours, or our mothers'. Dad even used to tell us it was okay not to do homework. We were really happy about that, but we now know that homework would have had its benefits. However, we never did any, because *he* went up to the school and told the teacher that we did enough work at school and *he* didn't see why we had to come home and do more. Dad told the headteacher that there was no point in giving us homework as we would not be doing it. What about the kids who are sexually or violently abused? Do you think they're sitting there remembering what the teacher is teaching them? I think not. They have more pressing things to think about.

I don't know who made the rules about who should be privileged and who should not. Why should some people live a life of luxury while others struggle endlessly? How unfair is that? Why should someone like me work until I'm exhausted for a few pounds while others do very little for thousands? I don't care if you're a footballer or a film star—if you choose that profession and love it, yes, you should get good money. But why is it when I go out to work a job I don't particularly like, yet still do to the best of my ability, I go home shattered and fed up because yet another day of people showing their authority over me, treating me like dirt just because I'm in a lower grade and hardly get enough pay to live on?

How vulgar of you people, and how do those factors give you the right to treat any human with disrespect, especially if they're doing everything right in life? How can you justify it? You can't, and you don't care to either. One day, I hope we get a government that will have fairer rules, so we can all enjoy a bit of luxury, decent food, and entertainment. We should all be able to send our kids to after-school activities to see what they are best at and what they want to do. If people were paid a decent wage, there would be less crime, less sadness, less anger and more children would grow up to be better people. What the hell do people expect the poor to do when they're starving? If the poor shoe was put on the rich foot, I wonder how they would like it.

Of course, it was Maggie Thatcher who decided it would be best for the country to allow landlords to charge whatever price they liked. What a stupid cow. She was part of this country's downfall. The government also allows employers to pay shit wages while rents are high. It's just ridiculous. Thousands of people work hard all week and still have to visit a food bank, but landlords can buy whatever they want because they're robbing the poor. It's the Robin Hood story, isn't it? I don't know how they sleep at night, they should be ashamed of their uncaring attitude towards their fellow human beings.

So, Brad and I stayed in the B&B for about a year, and then we heard of a cottage that was up for rent. It was one of three on a farm about three miles away from the B&B, but it was secluded. We were basically living in the middle of fields. That's all it was—just endless fields and a country path. The surroundings were beautiful, but the cottage was a bit of a disaster and needed renovation.

It still had open fireplaces in all the rooms. There was a bedroom downstairs and an attic upstairs. The attic ceiling was falling apart, and there were only bare floors made of untreated wood. There was no furniture, only a fridge and a cooker in the kitchen. Oddly enough, the toilet and shower room were also in the kitchen. It was a mess, and we had no money to do anything with it, but we were fed up with living with other people.

I had gotten a new job as a waitress in a Beefeater restaurant only about a mile from the cottage, so that was another reason to move. We decided to give it a go and moved into the cottage. It was quiet and tranquil. It wasn't easy getting to work as neither of us could drive. It was about half a mile down the road to the bus stop, and then the bus took me the other half mile. The restaurant was a big house set in lovely grounds.

The interior of the restaurant was lovely, but then it became tacky when they had us waitresses dressed in Beefeater costumes. We had to wear a white puffy shirt with a frilly collar and a red and yellow pinafore with a red and white apron. At first, we looked ridiculous and felt ridiculous, but as time went on, we got used to them and didn't mind wearing them. The public quite liked them as well.

It was good I got that job as we were skint again, poverty-stricken once more. Our relationship was starting to crack as he wouldn't or couldn't stop drinking and refused to get a job. He didn't believe in working. He said the government forces people to work, which is right - you are forced to work if you want any kind of life. Everyone needs money. There's not an option, you either have a job and make a life for yourself, or you don't, and you have no life. So, I worked. Brad said I shouldn't.

"And what the hell are we supposed to do if neither of us is working—eat fresh air?" I questioned.

"Because that's about all we would be able to afford."

The job was really busy. I picked it up in no time and became good at it. We all kept our own tips, so every shift, you would come away with some money in your pocket, and then we got paid at the end of the week as well. Of course, it was a pittance, but it was much more than social money. Brad was on sick benefits by this time. He was still getting that paid, and the rent on the half-derelict cottage we were living in. Between the two of us, it was just enough to live on. But he was still drinking and that cost money—money we didn't have.

Sometimes he only needed enough for a pint, and the rest of the night he would sing and play his mouth organ, creating a party atmosphere and then people were more than happy to buy him drinks. That's how good a singer he was.

We went to Turkey for a holiday. We were in an open-air bar with flowers growing on the trellis ceiling, and the petals falling onto the table. It was so nice. There was a singer with a guitar who was pretty boring. When he went off for a break, Brad asked "Hey man, can I play a couple of songs?"

The bar owner said yes.

The bar was situated on a busy street in Bodrum. Brad started to sing and play the harmonica, and within a minute, people were gathering around in the street. By the time he finished, there were crowds of people clapping and whistling. He did another two songs, and the street was full of people. It was amazing! I thought that proved how talented he was. He was an intelligent, confident guy. Anything he did, he put 100% into it and became perfect at it. He taught himself the harmonica, and when he mastered that, he went on to the guitar and taught himself to play blues and some Spanish guitar.

He was the same at school, everything he tried, he practised until he was good, if not perfect, at it. He was a perfectionist. He was soft-hearted and wasn't scared to cry, but he could also be angry and aggressive. He knew how to fight and argue. He loved an argument.

Brad had a strong personality, very hard to break down, a bit like a horse, although eventually, you can break a horse—but not Brad! He spent months looking into religion, trying to understand it and what good it does, or not, as it may be. The fact is, he told me, there's a lot of death, cruelty, and unrest caused by religion. Some religions make you pay for the pleasure of worshipping an invisible god. The Mormons take 10% of your pay if you're stupid enough to give it to them. Scientology takes every last penny you have. You'd have to be really stupid to allow that. The Jehovah's Witnesses just let people die if the treatment they need doesn't comply with their rules. We were brought up with Christianity because it was the nearest church to us. Dad wasn't religious and neither was Mum. What I gathered from learning about the Bible was that it says to be good, not bad.

Look folks, if you need to believe in something, believe in yourself. That's what I do, and I haven't killed or tortured anybody, starved people, or burnt their homes. So, what do you say? Why don't we kick religion into next week and get rid of it? He also looked into Nostradamus' writings, trying to figure out what his writings were trying to predict.

Brad was quite an intelligent guy. He had a lot of knowledge, but he thought he knew it all—except for one thing he didn't know: butterfly cakes are the ones that have the top made into wings, not fairy cakes.

His mother told Brad that the butterfly cakes were called fairy cakes and the wings were fairy wings. I know for a fact that a fairy cake is just a cupcake, and the butterfly ones had the top sliced off, cut in half, and butter icing put on top of the cake. The two pieces of cake from the top are placed on the icing to look like wings.

Brad never liked to be proved wrong because, like all men, Mr. Know-it-all's think they are always right when in fact they're mostly wrong. Brad was kind, he loved kids and animals, and loved his mum and dad dearly. His dad tried very hard to get him off the drink, but he wouldn't even listen to him. His dad was a good man, a hard worker. He'd started as a miner working down the pits for a few years and then went into sales to sell the girders for the mines. He was a good salesman. The more he sold, the more money he made, and he made a lot of it. He was kind as well. He would take us out for dinner if he was in our area, (they lived in Newcastle), but he would be in Scotland often. Eric was so successful, that he could never understand why his son was the way he was, being drunk all the time, not working, not looking after me in any way, shape, or form. Mind you, Brad couldn't look after himself, never mind me.

The cottage wasn't working out, it was too far away from everybody and everything. We had to walk about a mile to the nearest shop and then back again, uphill. The place wasn't going to get renovated—not by us, anyway.

We didn't have two brass farthings to rub together. Brad decided he was going to see about getting a house from the council. He got an appointment and they said he would qualify for a house because he had his son, whom he saw most weekends. That put him quite far up the list, but it still took a few months. In the meantime, we moved out of the cottage and back up to the house beside Mum. We had been together now for nearly four years and things weren't getting any better with him. He was still coming home drunk when he could escape with some money to the pub. He wasn't a happy drunk most of the time. When he did come home happy, the smile would be wiped off his face right away, because I would be waiting to get onto him, and it would turn into an argument, sometimes ending in me leaving. I used to leave all the time but I always went back. He wasn't violent towards me, I wasn't scared of him, but every time he got drunk it made me angry because I was working most of the time we were together and he was spending his benefits and my money on drink. The longer it went on, the more resentful I got.

We had been at Mum's for about a year when Brad was offered a top-floor flat. It takes about ten years in this day and age, and if you're single it'll take twenty to get an allocation. The problem in this country with housing is all the houses go to the junkies, the drunks, the single mothers—not to people like me, who work hard, pay rent and council tax. But that's not good enough, it seems, they'd rather give houses to people who can't pay anything, make a mess, and damage the houses. I mean, what the fuck kind of society is that? It punishes the people who are doing everything right and gives everything to the people who are doing everything wrong, including breaking the law. It doesn't make sense, and it never will.

Why is it that your ordinary working class, who don't get paid a lot of money, have to pay ridiculously high rents from their small wages that, no doubt, they've worked hard for? Once they've paid the greedy landlord more than half their pay, there's not much left. And when people say sometimes during winter months they have to make choices between eating or heating, they really mean it. It does happen. It's so sad and downright wrong. These are the kinds of things Brad opened my eyes to, amongst many other things.

As I said before, he was politically minded. He spent a lot of time watching politics on TV and watching documentaries on many different things. He also read books. He taught me a lot about a lot. I was a different person when we split. I wasn't the quiet, empty-headed female anymore. After the grief of us splitting forever, I bounced back a few weeks later, stronger, confident, and ready to take on anybody that got in my way—a bit like a phoenix rising from the ashes. For the first time, my life was free of men. I was my own person and no one was going to take that away from me.

Eventually, we moved into the flat. It was alright, but it was a top-floor flat in a housing scheme, and not in a street that was not the best. But what choice did we have? We didn't have much, but we made it home. Nothing changed with Brad and his drinking. I gave up my job in the restaurant as it was too difficult to get there. I got another job in a local restaurant, it didn't pay much. He was spending the money as quickly as I was making it—the bastard. I was starting to think

'this is going to be my life with him. But how can I leave him?'

Brad was a mess, he couldn't look after himself. If it wasn't for me, the place would be a tip. There'd be no food in the house, and he wouldn't eat properly. I think I wanted to leave, but I felt trapped, as I felt I couldn't leave him to his own devices.

Weeks went by, he was still drinking and lying, promising he would stop. I'm sorry, but that's not good enough. I knew it wasn't good enough, but I didn't act on it. Even after everything he was putting me through, I still didn't want to break up. I just kept thinking that something would work when I found it. The band split up, mainly because of his drinking and Tam, the guitarist, was an arsehole. The drummer and the bass player were just fed up with the both of them, so they all decided to go their separate ways. This was a disaster as I was their biggest fan. I loved going to gigs, they were a really good blues band and every gig was full of people dancing and having a ball. It was a real shame. I think it was inevitable because Brad was out of control and I was losing control of our relationship.

Then a little ray of sunshine came to our attention one day. Someone we knew had a border collie pup that was looking for a home. She was adorable—how could we say no? They dropped her off one night. Brad was out drinking as usual. I never really knew how alone I was until I got that little dog. She was cute and gorgeous, she just wanted to bite my hand and play. She really cheered me up when I was on my own and angry. It all left me when she arrived that night. He came in three hours later, pissed as a fart. I didn't want a row that night—not that I ever wanted a row, but that's just the way it was. Our life was just one big row. We named the puppy Kim. We both loved her right away. She was a good distraction from all the shit that was going on.

Now we were going to go out walking every day. At that time, I was about 25 years old and didn't really like walking. We had gone for a couple of walks before we had the dog. I did enjoy them but wouldn't want to do it every day at that time. I was still working in the restaurant but was struggling to hold it down. It was shit money anyway. I was slowly going into a depression of despair. Not only did I have an adult child to cook and clean for, I now had Kim as well. I didn't mind the dog, because dogs are amazing animals. She kept me sane. The walking did too. I became a really good walker. I ended up doing most of the walks, even when I got home at times from work and he would be out drinking or lying drunk on the couch or the floor and the dog hadn't been out, only to do the toilet. Needless to say, that pissed me off. She was a border collie, for God's sake. That breed needs knackering every day, but the selfish drunk arsehole didn't care. Giving himself liver cirrhosis was more important. Eventually, I left the restaurant when I'd finally had enough. I was so fed up with everything.

I just couldn't cope any more, going to work and having to pretend my life was great and I was so happy smiling and being nice to people. It was just too hard, so I quit. Brad didn't care that I quit, he didn't like me working anyway. He didn't mind if I was on the social like him, but I could only go on benefits for a certain time, as it was not good. I had nothing to do most of the time and no money to spare. Nope, it wasn't for me, so I started to look for another job.

I saw an advert in the evening news for a silver service waitress for the executives of one of the banks in Edinburgh.

This looked interesting. I had only done silver service a few times before, so wasn't that experienced.

Invoice

Chapter Nine
The Bank Job 1990 -1992

The day of the interview arrived. I was on the bus, thinking that if I got this job, I wasn't going to let him ruin it for me. I was nervous because I really wanted the job. I walked into the revolving doors and found myself in a massive lobby with a huge round desk and three security guards in the centre. They instructed me to take the lift to the second floor; the office was on the left-hand side, and it was incredibly plush. The carpets were deep-pile, and there were large portraits of men in wigs and tights on the walls. The lifts were all mirrored inside.

As the lift door opened, I stepped into a lobby with four doors. I was directed to the left, and as I turned the corner, I saw a large room with giant, heavy wooden doors that resembled something from a haunted castle. A very long table could easily seat about forty people, and three smaller rooms could accommodate about eight people. It all seemed quite posh for me; maybe I would be too common for a place like this. But then I thought, why not me?

I took a deep breath, stood up straight and rooster-like, pushed my chest out. I was positive and ready to tackle this interview head-on. I was determined to get this job. As I walked towards the office, a good-looking girl walked by me. She had dark, silky straight hair and big brown cow eyes. She looked like one of the waitresses. I reached the office door and knocked. Someone shouted, "Come in." I opened the door and walked in to see a little white-haired lady, probably in her sixties, sitting at the desk.

"Hi, I'm here for an interview for the waitress position," I said,

"Oh yes, come in and sit down."

She asked all the usual questions and then told me about the job, the hours, the holiday entitlement and then showed me around. It was just after lunch, so the staff were still clearing away. The banquet room was amazing with its mile-long table and three big chandeliers glittering over it. It was an amazing room. The smaller rooms were nice too; they had nice chandeliers as well. It looked amazing, and I thought I would love to work here. So, I did everything I could to impress her. I looked extremely interested in everything she said and expressed my delight at how nice everything was and how this would be a step up from just waitressing in restaurants. I was sure I could do the job to the standard they were looking for. I was impressed with my performance and I think she was as well, but you can never really tell what they're thinking. All the way home, I was just praying and hoping I got it. This was a good job, one that would make a difference in my shit life. She said to call back in a couple of days to find out if I'd been successful.

Two days later, I went down to the phone box at 9:30 to phone and find out if I'd got the job. I was shaking a bit because I knew how I would feel if I didn't get it. It wouldn't be good. I dialled the number I'd been given and waited for an answer. Someone picked up the phone and said, "Hello." This was it, the moment of truth. Was my life going to get better or worse? It all came down to one word: yes or no. She said, "Your interview was successful, and I would like to offer you the job."

O.M.G! I did it. I got the job. Obviously, I said yes, I wanted it so much. I walked away from the phone box stunned, high as a kite. It was an amazing day, and the sun was shining too. Now, I had to tell Brad the good news. When I did, he said, "Well done," even though he didn't want me to have a job. I didn't care what he thought anymore. This was a chance to get back on our feet. I was to start the following Monday.

The weekend went quickly, and before I knew it, Monday morning was here. I got the earlier bus to make sure I was on time. As I approached the 10-foot solid wood doors, I couldn't believe I was going to walk through them to start another episode of my life. When I went into the staff room, no one was there yet, so I changed into my uniform and waited.

The first to arrive was the girl I had seen at my interview. She said, "Good morning, my name is Eileen."

I said, "I'm Evette, good to meet you."

Next to come in was a thin, short blonde-haired girl named Maria, and then a tall dark-haired girl named Janice. They all seemed nice, and there was Danny. He was Margaret's son-in-law and the chef.

The first shift went well. It was like nothing I had done before. We were serving meals to some top executive bankers. They were just men in suits to me. I'm a bit wary of men in suits as the *monster* always wore a suit. It was not just that, though. Men who wear suits to work are usually pompous, intimidating dickheads because they get paid enormous sums of money for whatever they do sitting behind their desks. Having said that, however, I do like a man in a suit at a wedding.

The shift went well. We served lunch to the eight bankers. The girls were serving at another dinner that night, but I was going home at 3 as it was my first shift. I said goodbye to them and headed off for the bus home. As I walked to the bus stop,

I felt happy and felt a sense of security. I knew I was going to like the job.

When I got in, Brad wasn't in—what a surprise. The dogs hadn't been walked, and the house was left like a tip with dirty dishes lying about. Of course, I knew where he was: the fucking pub.

I had to set to, tidying up, washing his dishes, and taking the dogs out after working all day, while he was as free as a bird, doing what he wanted, as usual. I had done this many a time and I was getting tired of it. Brad was growing more selfish by the day. I was starting to despise him, and he was turning into a man that I didn't want.

The next time I was at work, it was to serve dinner in the evening as well. I was getting to know the staff a bit better. I liked Eileen a lot. She was so easy-going and had a wicked sense of humour, a bit like me. We finished the lunch service at about 2:30, and I went to the shops to have a look at what I could buy when I got my first pay packet. I got back at about 3:45 and got changed, and the other girls rolled in just after me. They were giggling away, and Eileen's eyes were looking a bit glazed. They were eating everything in sight. I thought ' hello, there's something odd here.'

The next two shifts were the same, but now I had figured it out. The glassy eyes, the laughing and the munchies—I would bet my bottom dollar they're smoking weed. It could only be that. I thought' They're not getting away doing that without me!' I asked Eileen, "Where do you lot go in the afternoon?" She said, "We sometimes go up Arthur's Seat in the car or go around the shops, but mostly up Arthur's Seat."

"I was just wondering because you always come back happy and glassy-eyed and eating everything in sight." I said, "There's only one thing I know of that gives you all that."

"Do you smoke?" she asked,

I knew what she meant by that, and I said,

"Yes,"

We both just laughed and I said,

"Well, I hope I'm invited to go with you next time." She said,

"Of course you can come. Now we know you're one of us!"

So we would all go up to Arthur's Seat when we were on at dinner time, sit in the car, and get stoned before returning to work.

We never looked like we were taking anything, so we got away with it. It was risky, but I think we enjoyed the buzz of it. Our job was in the main building, but they had two other buildings just doors away, that also hosted lunches and dinners.

Almost every day, at lunchtime, we would have to take sandwiches to at least one of the places. We would take a joint with us, and after we dropped them off, we would run down one of the quiet side streets and smoke it there, in our uniforms and then go back stoned to serve lunch. It never affected our work, except once, on a Friday.

Fish was on the menu. Danny made fried lemon sole in breadcrumbs on a Friday, it was very popular with the bankers and with us. We all wanted the fish if there was any left. When we served it on a Friday, we were always willing the diners to take the other dish that was offered so there would be enough fish for our lunch. Nine times out of ten, we got our fish on a Friday.

Then came the fateful Friday. The way we served was that we put the plate down first on the table in front of the diner and then you put the fish on a platter to serve it on the plate.

On that Friday, I forgot to put the plate down first, so when I went to put the fish on his plate, there was no plate to put it on. Luckily, I'm a quick thinker in an emergency, so I just pivoted around to the hot plate, put the fish on a plate, and just plonked it down in front of him. He never noticed because he was busy talking. This made me a bit wary after that, and I didn't make any more mistakes. It didn't stop us smoking. We would smoke in doorways and hidden areas within the very old buildings.

Eventually, Shaila got a job there too. She's not into drugs but smokes cigarettes like a chimney. She came with us in the afternoons when we were all on. She would sit in the car as the car filled up with the fragrant smell of hash, not weed. In those days, it was all hash. There was hardly any weed. It was a treat if you could get your hands on it. We would go back to work and eat peanuts and chocolate. Sheila used to get passive smoking munchies too.

One night we were all on. There were toilets down on the second floor and we discovered that the end toilet had a window that opened which meant we could go there to have a smoke when we were serving dinners. There were offices above and below us, so no one was working at that time. We told Shaila that we were going to the toilets. She said, "OK," so off we trotted to the toilets. We went to the last one, locked the door, opened the window, and then sparked it up. We had a couple of draws each, and then we heard the door opening. We froze stiff, wondering who the fuck that was. The person mumbled something and then walked back out. We started to breathe again. We decided it was too risky to light it back up again. Eileen said, "Do you think they smelt it?" and

I said, "Probably, but never mind that. They'll be wondering what two females are doing in a toilet together, apart from smoking dope." We sprayed the air freshener and then scurried back up.

We told Shaila what had happened, and she burst out laughing, telling us that it was her who came into the toilets to put the shits up us.

What a relief that was! I could have killed her at the same time, but we ended up laughing about it. We were always playing pranks on each other. A few months later, they were looking for an assistant for the butler. Cameron applied for the job and got it. It was turning into a right family affair. Everything was going great with the three of us there. We laughed a lot, and then one day, bang, something very unexpected happened.

Eileen came into work one morning in tears and angry. She told us that someone had phoned her house the night before and was just putting the receiver down when she answered. She couldn't think who was doing this and why. We told her to get the number of the redial, 1471, and see if she recognized the number. The next time it happened that night she did that and in the morning when Eileen told us who it was, we couldn't believe it. It was Margaret, our manager. We couldn't figure out why. Then we remembered that Eileen had a little run-in with her about something stupid. I can't remember exactly what it was, but she didn't deserve what came next.

Margaret was phoning Eileen's house and just hanging up at least 5/6 times a day, and after the fourth day, Eileen had enough. So she phoned the police. It was distressing enough with the calls, but at that time, Eileen's aunt was in the hospital dying of cancer, so every time the phone rang, they would think it was the hospital with bad news. The police went and spoke to Margaret and of course, she denied it and said Eileen was making it up. Margaret was off work at this time on suspension because the company brought the auditors in and they found several things wrong with the books. They'd suspended her and left Danny in charge.

The question now was, how was he going to react to Eileen phoning the police? Well, we got that answer the next day when Eileen came into work and went to the office to speak to him about it. He wouldn't talk to her. He said he wouldn't discuss it. We found this a bit odd as we still had to work there. He knew it was true because he knew what a vindictive cow she was, and he knew that it was her who made the calls, but he couldn't take our side against his wife's mother. She'd have his guts for garters. He cut Eileen's hours and hours because we were siding with her. But what we didn't expect was Cameron siding with Danny because Danny knew what we were saying was true. What a traitor! Going against his sisters, knowing that they were the ones telling the truth. That was hard to swallow. You may ask why he did that. The answer was simple, he didn't want to lose his job.

Unfortunately, money comes before loyalty and that is very disappointing. Danny was cutting our hours and giving them to Cameron and Irene and anyone else he could persuade to come in. It was blatantly obvious what he was doing but he didn't care that he was ruining our lives, and worse, Cameron was helping him. We decided we weren't going to stand for it, so we agreed we were going to leave, but leave with a bang.

Every month they had a day when all the executives met in the big boardroom for lunch. There would be about thirty people there, plus Danny and Cameron. When that day arrived, we were ready for battle. In the morning, we did what we normally did. The plan was to walk out just before service because that would cause the most disruption, and that's exactly what we did. Eileen went into the office with us behind her to tell him we were leaving now, and he could stick the job up his arse. That was the first time any of us had walked out on a job. It felt good that we were brave enough to do it, but on the other side of the coin, we were unemployed again. That was a bit worrying, but it felt good to stand up to them.

That day we went straight to a lawyer to discuss taking them to court. He reckoned we had a case against them as long as we had a witness to back our version of events. The only person we could think of was Bella, the kitchen assistant. She hated Margaret and didn't like Danny much either, so we asked her if she would stand as a witness for us. She said she would because what he was doing was wrong. We had a case as long as we had a witness. Finally the day came for the court case. Me, Shaila, and Eilleen arrived and just behind us came Danny and our traitor brother. I still can't believe he stood against us and lied, because he knew damn well what had really happened. He had put himself first and lied, to keep his job.

Bella changed her mind too and didn't turn up, so that weakened our case. We didn't have much hope of winning, and a couple of weeks later, we got a letter saying just that—we had lost the case. It wasn't a surprise to lose it, but it was disappointing. Now we were all without jobs, and what the fuck were we going to do next?

A few weeks later, we were still jobless. I got an Evening News and noticed they had a job section. As I looked through the vacancies, I saw a part-time job for a kennel maid at a cattery about a mile down the road. I thought it looked interesting. I love animals so I thought I would phone them and see what it was all about.

I phoned the next day, and a rather posh woman answered. I asked her what the job entailed, and she said it was cleaning the cats' boxes out. She also had a kennel with small dogs that she bred, that needed cleaning too. I asked her about the wage. It was £3.50 an hour—not a lot, but it was 1995. It was a pittance compared to what I was making at the bank, but it was better than nothing. We made a date for an interview two days later.

Two days later, I set off down the mile-long road walking with my two collies. I didn't know what to expect when I got there. The owner had sounded posh—maybe she would think I was too common for her. As I approached the house, I could hear dogs barking, and I thought I'd obviously got the right place. The dogs were tied up on the big metal gate that separated the cattery from a piece of land that was just all grass but had three big garages in it. In front of me was a bungalow with a staircase of about eight stairs leading up to a metal gate with an actual bell with the dinger inside, with a little rope attached to it. I thought that was really old-fashioned and I rang it. It was quite loud, but with several dogs barking, I didn't know if she would hear it inside, and I was right—no one answered. I rang it again and again. Third time lucky—a little blonde-haired woman came out of the front door. She was only about five feet in height and a bit plump. As she got closer, I noticed she had an overbite and it made her look a bit horse-like. I also noticed she had nice blue eyes and very good skin. Her shoulder-length hair was really thick too. She spoke in a nice, gentle way. She opened the gate and introduced herself—her name was Ellie. She seemed nice enough. As we approached the door, there were three little puppies in a pen at the side of the door—they were the cutest things I had ever seen. I was overwhelmed by their cuteness. She told me they were Pomeranians, "Poms" for short. I had never seen these dogs before, but I was about to see a whole lot more when she took me into the kennels.

The smell of shit hit me as we entered the kennels. There were about twenty dogs in there—most of them were Poms. There was also a Cavalier with three puppies and a Westie. The place stank, but there was a lot of cuteness going on. Ellie showed me around the cattery. It only had twelve pens, but there were soon going to be another twelve. I quite liked the idea of working with animals. After all, it couldn't be any worse than working with humans.

Ellie took me into the house—it was quite small inside. It had a big sitting room at the front that looked out to the main road. There was a double bedroom facing the front and at the back were two single rooms. One of them she used as her sitting room/office where she would do her work and watch TV.

The big room, Ellie told me, was only used for visitors. We seemed to hit it off right away—we had similar personalities and we made each other laugh. She could see that I loved animals and saw how much I loved my collies. She said she would let me know in a couple of days what her decision would be.

I waited for four days and she hadn't been in touch. I said to Brad, "I suppose I can't have got that job after all."

He said,

"Why don't you phone her and ask her if she has made a decision yet?"

I thought that was a bit forward.

He said, "What have you got to lose? You think you haven't got it anyway."

"I suppose so." I said.

When I phoned and said that I was just wondering if I had got the job, she said she had been going to give me a call today and offer me the job. I said yes right away—I would love the job. She said, "Okay, come down on Monday morning at 9:30."

"See you then!" I said gleefully, I couldn't believe it—I was so happy. This was a new kind of job, a challenge. I didn't know then just how challenging it would become.

Monday morning came, and I headed down to my new job with all, those cute animals to look after. I was looking forward to it. I rang the bell, but Ellie didn't hear it. I rang again and again and finally, she came round from the back.

"Good morning," she said. She unlocked the padlock and opened the gate. She said, "I'll show you what to do first."

We went up to the cattery, and she showed me what to do—how to clean out a cabin and sweep a run, and also scoop out pee and poo from the litter box. Well, the job seemed easy enough until we went down to the kennels. She opened the door, and the smell of shit was overwhelming. The noise of twenty dogs barking was also overwhelming—it was pandemonium.

In the kennels, I was to put all the dogs out to the runs and then clean the kennels. I had to lift the newspapers up off the floor and put them in a big black bucket. The papers were covered in shit and piss and all had to be put in the black bin. Then I had to mop the floors and put clean sheets of newspaper down before letting the dogs back in. Once I let them back in and shut the hatches down, then I had to go out to the runs and pick up the shit there and hosed the runs down. Admittedly, it did involve a lot of shit, and it was mostly a shit job, but the animals made up for it. I was doing it for them and their comfort. I didn't really agree with breeders because they lock their animals in cages and only care about the money they make from them. This was true of Ellie.

I didn't agree with it, but Ellie was not going to stop, so, I figured, I might as well be there for the animals. As long as I was there, they would be okay. At the end of my first shift, she asked me what I thought and if I would want to take the job. I said,

"Yes, I would." I told her.

"Well, I'll see you tomorrow then." she said.

As I walked down the road, I was happy for a change. My new job brought a little bit of happiness to my so-sad life. As usual, I didn't know what to expect when I got home. He didn't have any money to go drinking, but that hadn't stopped him in the past. I got in, and he was in.

"How did it go?" he asked,

"Good, I think I'm going to like it."

Brad asked about Ellie, what she was like. I said she seemed nice.

"She's got a good sense of humour!" I said, "We spoke about family and things to get to know each other. I think we're going to get on well."

A week passed and Ellie and I were getting on great. I found out she was 16 years older than me, but she did not look it. If anything, she looked about the same age as me. Her skin was amazing—fair, not a blemish on it, and she had thick blonde hair. She'd never married or had kids. We were similar there because I hadn't done either too. As time went on, we became friends. We got on so well, we would talk about everything. She was a very intelligent woman and a very successful one too. We started to go to the cinema and the theatre together. We would go out for the occasional meal as well and any shows that we fancied when the Edinburgh Festival was on during the summer.

Eventually, when she knew she could trust me and saw that I was competent, Ellie asked me if I would like to stay over one weekend and look after the business while she went to a dog show. She showed her Pomeranians at shows all over the country. She was very good at it; she won many shows in her time. She was also a very successful breeder of Poms. She had a very good bloodline and sold dogs all over the world.

I did my overnight stay and everything went well. It was quite good not having the boss around when I was working. It was during a quieter time in the year when there weren't so many cats in. The next time I did it was when she went to Crufts, which is around Easter time, and this time the cattery was full. That was much harder. It was backbreaking, but I got through it and did a good job for her. I loved the job, but it was only part-time, so it wasn't bringing in a lot of money.

I thought I should take on another part-time job. I saw one in a local restaurant that was a couple of miles down the road from the cattery. It was 20 hours a week, which was perfect.

I had experience in waitressing, so it didn't take much to snap the job up. I was to start the next weekend. I was mainly at the cattery Monday to Friday, so working at the weekend fitted in. I would have a couple of evenings on during the week as well. That was hard because I got home from the cattery at about 1:30 and started at the restaurant at 6pm. Sometimes I had to go down to the cattery if Ellie was away and wouldn't be back to let customers in to collect their cats or drop them off. If they came between 5 and 5:30 pm, that was fine. But any later and I started to panic because I was going to be late. Those days were very stressful, but somehow I always got there on time.

My boss at the restaurant was a little grumpy man. He was smaller than me, and I'm only 5'1", but he had a big bank account. His name was Ralph, and the restaurant was doing well. His brother owned another one a few miles up the road, and that was doing well too. I ended up working in that one as well a few years later.

Things weren't getting any better with Brad. At least now that I had the two jobs, I would be better off. We had been together for about 10 years by this time but he was going downhill set to self-destruct I couldn't be bothered anymore with the same old shit year in, year out. I wanted a better life, but it would be another 4 years before we split for good. I did still love him, but not the same as when we first met. He destroyed those feelings from my heart, and they'd never return. The last year, I was more or less his carer. We parted as friends, but even with the misery, it was hard to give up after 14 years. His life was going down the pan, but I wasn't going to let mine go down too. We finally split in September 1995.

After a few months, I was able to save some money. I was never able to save in the past because of him. It felt good having some extra money for a change. I didn't have a pathetic selfish bastard anymore, feeding off my emotions and spending my hard-earned cash. Yes, it felt good getting my identity back— to just be able to go out to work and not worry about what was going on at home and to come home to a clean, quiet house. It was so good. I made my mind up then that I was going to make a success of my life, what was left of it. I worked hard, but there wasn't enough money coming in. I thought about training in something else but couldn't think what. Cameron suggested floristry.

"Good idea, Cam," I said, " that sounds good. I've always wondered how they manage to get the arrangements to look the way they did." It was only a year's course, so I thought, 'Why not? I might be able to open my own shop.'

I told Ellie that I was leaving to do the course. She wasn't best pleased because she had come to trust me with her business. I told her that I would still be able to do weekends when she was away. She was happy about that but worried about finding someone else she could trust and who could do the job as well as I did. I already had the answer.

I said, "What about my sister Shaila?" I had only known Ellie for a couple of years, and she hadn't met Shaila yet, but she had met my mum. I told her Shaila was trustworthy, a very good worker, and an animal lover. She said, "She sounds like you," and

I said, "Yes, she's just like me, but I'm better looking!"

Shaila had been down to the cattery a couple of times to pick me up, and I had shown her around, and she loved the place. So when I told her I was leaving, she wanted the job. An interview was arranged, and Shaila got the job. When I went in the next day,

She said, "Your sister is so like you."

I said, "I told you so!"

I started my course, and Shaila started work down at the cattery. Ellie was very pleased with her and said it was just like having me there. The flower arranging was quite good. I did enjoy it, and I got the Student of the Year award because I hadn't done any flower arranging at all before the course, and my tutor said I had made the most progress. So I was now a qualified florist. My first qualification, it's only an SVQ 2, but I was happy to have it. I finally achieved something that had turned out well, and nobody could take it away from me. I never did open a shop.

A few months after doing the course, one of the students, Fay whom I got on really well with, phoned me and asked me if I'd want some part-time hours. She had opened a shop in Edinburgh. I said I'd love to, and it would give me a chance to see if I would like to do it for a living. I worked with her for about six months. I quite liked it. Working with the flowers was lovely, but it is a cold job for most of the time, and I can't stand the cold, so it went back on the back burner for another time.

So what next? It would have to be another job that paid good wages. One day I was speaking to my neighbour who lived in the top flat and worked for the university, cleaning student accommodation in Edinburgh. I was telling her that I was looking for another job, and she said they were looking for staff. She gave me the number of her supervisor and told me to call her. I did just that, got an interview, and got the job.

Chapter Ten
Mrs Porteous I Love You 1999 -2013

Mrs Porteous, who interviewed me and gave me the job, started my climb up the ladder. All I needed was a break, and that lovely, glorious woman gave it to me. I started the job. It was only a cleaning job, but the money was good, well, as good goes for a cleaning job. I worked at the weekend, and it was the weekend money, time and a half on Saturdays, double time on Sundays, and extra hours during the week that boosted my wages significantly. The job was cleaning the students' rooms most of whom lived like pigs. Their rooms were like tips. After two years there, I got fed up and moved on to the hospital, cleaning wards. It was the liver ward, probably the worst ward of them all. Lots of incontinence, verbal and physical abuse in there, people coughing up blood and people shitting out blood. The majority of the patients there are alcoholics, and because they haven't done a shit in two weeks, the toxins from the shit start to seep into the bloodstream and cause confusion. There are a lot of enemas given in the liver ward to get the shit out. It was a sad place to work in, seeing what alcohol does to a person, really quite disturbing. I knew that Brad was going down this pathway and possibly my brother as well. That made me sad.

I was a domestic for two years, and then I decided to buy the council flat we were in, but I wasn't earning enough to do that. It came about that the ward was looking for a Health Care Assistant, so I applied, and of course, I got the job. I got a loan to pay for the flat mum and I were living in and bought it. I suppose things were looking up. I was a homeowner!

I had no sooner bought the flat then the neighbours above me decided to start making noise late and through the night. There was a family up there: the mother, who was called Amy, and her partner Chaz. They had two teenage boys, one about 19 and the other 18. Chaz and Amy split up and she took up with another man. Amy moved out of the flat to live with him and left the boys there. So they both got new jobs in bars in Edinburgh, which finished late, and they thought it was okay to come home a few times a week with inebriated people at 2 in the morning. Needless to say, there was a lot of noise going on, thuds on the floor, running about, things being dropped on the floor - my ceiling. It was terrible. I was being kept awake and had to get up to go to work at 6 am to pay for the loan I had just taken out to buy the damn place.

I went up to speak to the mother, and that's when the boys told me she wasn't there, but they would be staying there. I asked them to stop the noise as it was keeping me and my mum awake. They said they would, but surprise, surprise, two nights later, once again, noise until 5 in the morning. Needless to say, I was raging. I had to take the next day off as I was shattered.

I couldn't do this anymore, twelve-hour shifts with no sleep. What the fuckin' hell was I going to do? I had just bought the damn place, and these little arseholes decided to make it impossible for me to live there. Another two weeks passed, and nothing changed. By this time, I was an extremely angry, tired zombie who just wanted to kill someone. A month went by, and they were still doing it. I phoned the police one night. They came out, but when they arrived, the little bastards had quieted down, so the police just left. There was no more noise that night, but a couple of nights later, it was back to the same old shit. This was now war. I had enough. I went to the council to complain. They said I'd have to keep a diary of when this was happening and try and get a witness to corroborate my complaint.

I was friendly with Rose, who was above them in the top flat, so I asked her if they were disturbing her. She said she didn't hear much from below. I told her what was going on, and she said she'd help if she could. I was still going to work, but I shouldn't have been. After being tormented for about six weeks, I was slowly going off my head with sleep deprivation.

Rose came to my door and said she had her dog out to go to the toilet at 5 am before getting ready for work and was horrified that she saw just what I had told her - people jumping up and down on a bed above my bedroom, and also people running about. She said she was going to the council to report to them that I was telling the truth and she saw it with her own eyes.

I was getting really worried because how much more could I stand? I'm only human, the same as them. What made them think I could carry on like that? It was so hard going out to work with hardly any sleep. I was becoming depressed and anxious. So one day at work, I had a run-in with one of the nurses about toast. The toaster in our kitchen wasn't working, so I said I'd go to the next ward's kitchen and make us toast. When I got there, the kitchen staff said that their toaster was also broken, but they had one in the pantry, so I went to the pantry.

It took ages to get it done as the toaster was very slow. After about 15 minutes, it was done. I hurried back to the staff room, and when I got back, they had decided they were having biscuits and cheese. I was a bit annoyed as I had spent half my break making the toast.

I just said, "Well, that's nice. I just won't bother next time." The nurse that I was mainly doing it for verbally attacked me, saying.

"You cannot talk to me like that, who do you think you are?"

That's all I needed, bad feeling at work as well as at home. I decided that was it. I was going to have to take time off. I got a line from my doctor for a couple of weeks off. Little did I know it would take almost three months to get all this fixed.

Let the battle commence.

As always, the minute you start to see light at the end of the tunnel, it starts to get further away before you can reach it. I was feeling down. There's always somebody wanting to make life difficult and hold me back. I thought about just giving up again. It would probably be easier just to lie down and be depressed and sad and let others take care of you, but to be honest, that's not me. I decided if they wanted to take me on they could bring it on! For starters, their flat still belonged to the council, so I could get them evicted. I just needed evidence against them. I got that evidence a few days later when my neighbour Rose came to my door.

The partying had stopped, but the creaking floorboards above were still annoying me. Anytime something was dropped on the floor, I could hear it. Even footsteps drove me crazy, so I decided to go to Turkey for a holiday. Brad and I had been there years ago and loved it, so Mum and I went, and again it was amazing. I got talking to an English woman who lived there. As we chatted she told me that her apartment was going up for sale for only 28 thousand euros. She took us to the apartment, which was nice, but only had one bedroom, although there was a small plunge pool. I took her email address and said I'd be in touch, but of course, I never did.

When I got home, I spoke to a Turkish nurse and she said she wouldn't advise living in Turkey. So if a Turkish person was telling me not to migrate to Turkey, I was going to listen and forget the idea.

I decided I couldn't stay in the flat any longer, so I started looking at the best options to get it sold, quickly. A few days later, a leaflet came through the door from a company saying they were looking for houses to buy at a fair price. They would arrange it all and pay the solicitors as well. All I needed to do was sign some papers, arrange a date, and move out. That day came on the 4th of April 2001, Mum and I moved out and into Dory's house down the road in a nice little village. She'd bought the three-bed house with a massive back garden before she left for the States with her husband Angus to set up a karate club. They had both been very active in martial arts in Dunfermline, and Dory and Angus were black belts. At least things seem to be going well for one member of the family!

For £400 a month, Mum and I were to stay in their house. We moved and were instantly £57,000 better off. That's what I got for it; it would have been at least 10 grand more if it was done up. However, I only paid 12 grand for it, so it was a pretty good profit, but 57 grand wasn't really a lot of money.

I had to spend some of it. Mum and I took ourselves off to Gibraltar, and a couple of months later, we went to Malta. I gave Shaila £2,000 to help clear her debts, and I gave her another £1,000 a few months later. I also gave Veronica and Stuart, Shaila's kids £500 each, and I sent £500 over to Dory to help her out as she was struggling at that time. I spent some on furniture for the house, some on clothes and makeup, some on three acid face peels, Botox and filler, and some of it I wasted on shit. Well hey-ho, I went from poor to rich within a month. I'd suffered poverty all my life and having that money was amazing, but it was going down fast, so I thought I would have to do something about it. I had to invest.

There was not much left after about a year of self-indulgence and stupidity, I had about £28,000 left, so I decided to invest £20,000. I invested it for six years in a half-bond, half-share investment, which meant that after the six years, I should have made some interest, but it didn't get calculated until the investment matured when the six years was up.

This particular investment guarantees that you don't lose any of the money you put in, no matter what happens with the stock market. I liked the fact that I wouldn't lose any money but only gain, although I had to wait six years to find out how much I would have.

I just continued working and tried to save a little bit at a time, but it wasn't working. I was struggling to make ends meet on my own. We also started going over to America more often, and that didn't help financial matters either. I was getting further into credit card debt because of the holidays. I had to find a way to make some more money. It was obvious. I had two rooms doing nothing, so I decided to rent at least one of them out. I advertised for a lodger, and after two or three disappointments, I found a Polish girl called Kashia. She was a student and was looking to move out of the place she was in. She was pleasant and polite and a happy person, but not too happy, because that would be annoying.

Kashia liked the place, and her boyfriend Greg lived just four doors down from me. I'd known him for years, he used to go about with my nephew when they lived here. He was a nice chap. So I thought I'd give her a go. She agreed to pay £200 a month, which was half the rent. She turned out to be a good lodger. Apart from an untidy room, she was alright. She stayed for over a year and then went to London to finish the rest of her course. She and Greg split up when she left. That was me on my own again. It didn't bother me; I like my own company, so I was glad to have the house to myself again. I thought, no more lodgers, I was just going to try and survive on my own.

A few weeks went by, and then Veronica had a bust-up with her boyfriend Billy. It was a bit of a brawl, but she fires people up that much you just want to punch her. I've had a couple of run-ins with her myself. Billy had nowhere to go, so Mum took him in for the time being, and then I ended up letting him stay. Billy was one of the good guys. He wasn't any trouble, but Veronica was mad that I had let him stay as she was wanting him to roam the streets and suffer. That's the kind of person she was back then and to be honest, still is but she's older now and not quite as bad. You cross her and you're damned to hell. She's her father's daughter because my sister's personality is nothing like hers.

Billy was with me for a few weeks, and I got nothing but abuse from her. I tried not to let her get to me normally, except for one night when she came down to my house wanting to batter Billy. It was a Sunday night, and I had been working the day before for 12 hours, and the same again on the Sunday. Needless to say, the last thing I needed when I arrived home on Sunday night at about 9 o'clock was her threatening to come down and cause trouble. I had a cup of tea and then took the dogs out for a walk.

At about 10 o'clock, and I had just got in the gate when she appeared out of her friend's car. It was a race between us to see who was going to get to the door first because I knew if she got in the house, it would be carnage. I managed to get through the gate before her and in my door, but she managed to get half her body in the door. I put the chain on and pressed the door, hoping it would hurt so she would back off, but nope, she was determined to get in. It was quite funny actually. She was trapped between the door and the door frame, and Billy and I were pushing the door shut so she couldn't get in any further. I whacked her hand with my phone to see if that would make her let go, but it didn't work. It was just getting ridiculous. We had been fighting for about 20 minutes so I said, "I'm phoning the cops!"

"Go ahead!" she shouted, so I did.

The police took about 15 minutes to turn up. It's pretty hard to keep someone out of your house when they're already halfway in the door. The officers removed her from the door. I don't think she thought I would really phone them, but I had no option. She wasn't going to go away, and she needed to learn that when I said, "I don't want you in my house," I meant it. She spent the night in the police station, and a few months down the line, she was taken to court and fined £500. She gave me no more grief after that, and we're in a better place with each other now. She's become an older, more balanced, and more reasonable person. What Veronica needs to realize is that being unreasonable, selfish, and greedy are not attributes that make people like you.

I ended up telling Billy he would have to move out as I couldn't have any more bother with Veronica as she obviously wasn't going to leave it, so he moved out, and all the aggro stopped. I didn't want anything more to do with her niece or not, that was the last straw. I didn't see her for months. I'm not being disrespected like that after all I've given her in the past and all the money I'd spent on the kids, taking them to the cinema costing £50 a time, and we went a good few times. They got the works. We would go on the bus to the swing park at the Meadows and then get a taxi to the cinema, pay a fortune to get into the cinema, then another fortune for ice cream, popcorn and juice and a taxi back to the park, then the bus home. I spent a lot of money and time on those kids, but it was never appreciated by her.

Billy went to stay with someone he had been speaking to on the web. After a few weeks, he got a temporary house, and about a year later, he got a permanent place, so it all worked out for the best in the end. After Billy went, I decided there would be no more lodgers. I just wanted my house to myself. I decided to look after dogs.

I decided to put a fence up to halve the garden and have the back bit left wild while the other half would be turfed and levelled for the dogs. I painstakingly shovelled countless wheelbarrows of mud, it was hard work, but I got there. It took a few days as I was doing it between shifts, but I did it. Next, the turf came delivered out the front. I had no idea that turf was so heavy, it took all my might to lift one piece and there were 20 of them! These are the problems you have when you don't have a bit of muscle in the house.

Luckily, my neighbour next door was a guy, far from a bit of muscle, but he was another pair of hands. Craig was a small, thin guy and he was from the criminal world. He sold weed and anything else he could get his hands on. He was no trouble at all. He saw me struggling and came out and gave me a hand. We lifted the turf onto the barrow and he wheeled it around, then we both lifted it off again. I was knackered afterwards it would have taken me ages to do that myself. He really helped me out. I bought him a couple of pouches of tobacco and he was happy with that. I still had a lot to do, the turf had to be laid and the fencing had to go up. I started looking into fencing but it was far too expensive. In the end, I put four posts up and got a massive roll of chicken wire that went right around the part of the garden I was going to use. I attached it to the fence that was around the garden already and onto the four posts I had erected, with Mum's help. Then I put bamboo screening all the way around as well. It did the job. Then Mum and I laid the turf, it almost killed her off and I wasn't far behind her. So the garden was ready, all I needed was some dogs to put in it.

The next task was to get some customers. I got some business cards printed and put them in the adverts box in the hospitals and also advertised on the net. It wasn't long before I started getting bookings. The first dogs I got were local, just up the road in fact. There were two: a male border collie called Max, who was scared when he was outside, got anxious when cars approached, and would just lie down until they passed. Then he would pull on the lead; this went on the whole walk. He was a lovely dog and the woman that owned him, whom I knew from work, loved her dog to bits. The other one was a little white and brown Jack Russell called Molly. She had a skin condition that flared up and made her itch. They weren't the perfect dogs for my first time but I said I would take them. It was only for a couple of nights. It all went well and the dogs went home just as they had arrived, happy and healthy. Their owner was very pleased and booked them in again. I couldn't be happier. I felt confident I was going to be able to do this.

My customer told her friend about me and then she started booking her two dogs in. Another anxious border collie, but I couldn't even get this one out the gate, though I tried every day. Her other dog was so cute. He was called Harry and had the softest fur and a little squishy face. He was so much fun as he was only 1 year old when he first came to me. This customer was a worrier and wouldn't leave her dogs with anybody, but she trusted me with them, and I had them many times.

Next I got two cocker spaniels in for a weekend. People were phoning, inquiring, and booking. My new venture took off quickly. I was asked by a male nurse if I would take his four greyhounds: three female ex-racers and one male greyhound cross that looked like a greyhound but was smaller than the females. I said I probably could. After I said it, I thought, "What have I done?" I had never looked after a greyhound before. All I knew about them was that they had long legs and ran fast. It would be a challenge but I was willing to give it a go. Four of them would bring in a good amount of money. We arranged a weekend to start with to see if I could manage. The boarding idea was great as I was getting in dogs that I never had in the past, a pug called Pugly and a little timid Chihuahua called Pippin. She was really scared when she first arrived and wouldn't come out of her little crate, that was her safe haven. Gradually, I got her to come out, and once she had come out and fully trusted me, she was great and full of fun.

The weekend came for the greyhounds to arrive. I was nervous because I had only been up and running for a couple of months. The guys drove up and I went out to meet them, as I did with all my customers. They had a big four-by-four. They opened up the back and all I could see were four heads on four long necks. They looked amazing. The guys got them out of the car and as we walked down the pathway, a cat appeared and they went mad, barking loudly, in a frenzy. We hurried them in the door. By the time all their bedding was put in the living room, I could hardly see any of the floor; it took up so much room. I took them out for walks two at a time, watching carefully for cats, but we didn't see any. When I decided to go to bed, I left them in the living room with the door open and I left my door open too so I could hear what they were doing. I was in bed a whole 5 minutes when I heard them stirring. I've got laminate flooring throughout the whole house and all I could hear was footsteps.

They were coming up the hallway, as they approached my door, they started to seek round my door four long heads attached to four long necks, and it looked like a mythical creature with four heads. They made me laugh and feel sorry for them so I got up, gave them a clap, and took them back up the corridor to the living room again, then went back to bed. Five minutes passed and once again they decided to try again and came up to my door. I couldn't send them away again. Instead, I went through and brought their four beds through to my room. I had a two-seater couch there, so whoever got on there first had that to sleep on. I had to let one of them on my bed, so I chose the male as he was the smallest. The other two had the bedding. So these were to be the sleeping arrangements for their stay. It was okay with me because I could keep an eye on them overnight. The weekend went well with them and when the guys came back to collect them, they were delighted. They booked them in for May that year for nearly three weeks. I was really glad it had worked out with them. They were really nice dogs, gentle and quiet. They truly are wonderful dogs, but they could shit for Scotland, England, Ireland, and Wales. I can honestly say I've never seen so much shit. The four of them did at least 3 piles a day each; it was bad, very bad. I had to get rid of bags of it every day.

The time from February to May went by quickly. Before I knew it, the greyhounds were back again. I knew it would be hard work but I was looking forward to the challenge. They arrived on a Friday. Everything was great on Friday and Saturday. We went out for walks 3 times a day, two at a time, so that added up to 6 walks a day. It was a lot but I had been walking my own dogs for years so I was used to it and walking had become a way of life for me. It felt weird if I couldn't get out for a walk. On Sunday night, I went out with Rosie and the male who was called Musky. I had a double chain that I had in the house. It was a small hoop with two chains attached so you can put two dogs on the one lead. So you then have two dogs on one lead. I thought this would be easier to control them. It was working well. We went to the park as it was getting dark. I walked around the park and then headed home.

I was approaching the gate when a cat ran out from under a car parked at my door. Rosie saw it and went mental, barking and jumping about. Through all the commotion, the lead was somehow knocked off the chain.

It was my worst nightmare come true. The two of them ran still chained together. I could just see their cute little arses running away from me. I was left with the lead in my hands and I started to run after them. Everything was going through my head when I was running, but I felt everything was in slow motion. I've experienced that before when one of my Pomeranians started to run towards the main road. I managed to catch her in time, but it's the weirdest thing. So I was running as fast as I could - after two greyhounds! Bearing in mind I am 50 years old now. As I was running, I was crying, thinking I didn't have a hope in hell of catching them. I got round the corner, and there they were. I don't know why they stopped. They didn't see me at first, so I quietly got behind them, and just as I reached out to grab hold of them, Rosie saw me and bolted over the road with Musky beside her. Just as they did that, a four-by-four that was stationary started to move. It was perfect timing Now I truly was in my worst nightmare. I grabbed hold of them and walked them off the road to the pavement. Rosie was limping. The guy in the car asked if she was okay. I said I couldn't see properly because it was too dark. I said, "Don't worry, I'll go home and see."

He drove off and in the panic, I didn't get any details. I just wanted to get her home. I knew she was bleeding. We walked around the road, and when I got her in, her leg was bleeding badly. I ran to the kitchen, got my first aid box and bandaged up her leg. I knew I had to get her to the vet quickly. I phoned a taxi and told them what had happened and I needed a taxi right away. The depot was just up the road away so they were there within 5 minutes. I phoned Mum and told her to come up for the other dogs and told her there was blood all over the floor, and I mean all over the floor. There was an emergency vet about 10 miles away. It seemed to take forever. The driver was an older man who used to have greyhounds, and he was really good with the situation. He waited for me without running the meter to take me back home. The vet came out and said she had severed a vein in her leg. It wasn't good; her leg was in a mess. She said this wound was going to take a long time to heal. She said months, maybe a year. This was devastating. How was I going to tell her owners all this? Now I was wishing I hadn't taken them. Maybe I've bitten off more than I could chew. I thought 'I'm finished before I had even started!' They kept her in overnight, and I went back home. Mum cleaned some of the blood up, and then she must have got fed up and left it. She'd got a taxi home before I got back.

Chapter Eleven
What the hell - just give up! 2013/2017

The other dogs were happy to see me so that was something. I got the mop bucket out and mopped the rest of the blood up, there was a lot of it. It was three in the morning before I got to bed. What a nightmare that was, and it wasn't over yet. I still had to tell the owners, who were in Cuba, and look after Rosie, as she recovered, for the next two and a half weeks.

Tomorrow came soon enough, and it was time to phone the owners. I couldn't get through to them, so I left a message. I phoned the vets, and they said Rosie had had a good night. She was on fluids, her leg had stopped bleeding and she could stand on it. I was to come and pick her up. I didn't have a car, so it would be two buses there and a taxi back. When I saw Rosie, I just burst into tears. Luckily, she had no other injuries; it was just her leg, so that was a Godsend. We got home in one piece. I used the same taxi company, and they were only too happy to help.

The first week, I was down at the vets every second day to get her dressings changed. It was a taxi there and back; it cost me £150 for all the journeys. I had to carry her up and down the stairs for the first week until she got her strength back. She was a big greyhound, but I found strength from somewhere to do the best for her and the other three.

I must have phoned the owners half a dozen times, but they never replied. I couldn't think why, this was the number they gave me. It was a mystery, so I just carried on caring for Rosie, thinking they would get back to me eventually.

The insurance company was amazing. They believed my story right away. They didn't ask for the driver of the car's details, which was a bit of a surprise to me. That was just as well as I didn't have them. I think it cost them well into five grand for her treatment, and they paid it no problem. I had £50 excess to pay. By the time I'd deducted the £200 for the taxis and insurance, I was only left with £100 for my trouble. It was hard work for £100, but I was just pleased that Rosie was alright and her leg was healing up well.

The dog's time with me was almost up. The owners were due back in the morning. They still hadn't been in touch. It puzzled me because I was sure they loved those dogs and would want to know if anything was wrong. Anyway, I was going to find out in the morning.

The next day was a beautiful spring day. The dog's owners were landing at noon, that's if they were even coming back. I didn't know what had happened, they had not answered my calls and messages.

I waited to hear from them or to see them, whatever came first. The phone rang about 12:30; finally, it was them. I told them what had happened, and they were shocked. They couldn't believe it; they weren't expecting this bad news as soon as they got off the plane.

They arrived at the house about an hour later, and the reason they hadn't got my calls was because they couldn't use their phone there, and I didn't have them on social media. They were actually alright about it all when I told them what had happened and what I had to go through to look after Rosie and the other three and when they realised the money I had spent. I told them that I didn't know if I should or even wanted to continue with the boarding because I couldn't go through anything like that again. But they were really supportive and said they could see it had been an accident. They said if Rosie wasn't the way she was with small furry animals, it wouldn't have happened. They wanted to book them in again for September for a couple of weeks. I was really surprised that they were so understanding. So, I thought, well, if they believed it was a fluke and I wasn't at fault, why shouldn't I carry on?

I said, "Okay then, I'll take your booking and thanks very much!" When they left, I just flopped on the couch, shut my eyes, and thought 'thank goodness they've gone. It had been a long two and a half weeks.

I did carry on. They came back in September, and everything went great. They booked them in the year after that and the year after that, and that year there was almost another disaster.

When Shaila came to stay, she took them out with me. When I was on my own, I took them out in twos, but when she started walking with me, we went out with all four of them. Most of the time, it went without a hitch.

We live opposite quite a long main road with houses on both sides of it. Our street has a big bit of grass and trees before you reach the main road, and on the other side of the road, there is also grass and trees running up the side of the road all the way up to the top.

We decided to walk them up this road because we could see if any other dogs were coming, so we had plenty of warning so we could turn back or cut up another street. Most of the time, it was okay because they were okay with bigger dogs.

But if anybody appeared with a little dog, Rosie would want to chase it as she would a cat. It wasn't her fault, it was what she had been trained to do in her racing life. It was a lovely sunny day and we headed out with them. We got across and headed up the road. We didn't get far when I saw a big brown dog at the top of the street. I said to Shaila,

"I hope there's someone with that dog up there." She saw it and said, "So do I," but to our horror, it was running down with no human and no lead. Oh my God, it was heading right down towards us! Panic set in. I shouted, "About turn and run!"

We ran with them over the busy road; we had no choice. The big brown dog was getting closer, and he had seen us, he was coming for us.

Cars had to brake, they could see what was unfolding in front of their eyes. We ran into a garden that had four steps from the gate down. Shaila ended up falling down the stairs, and I ran down them with the dogs following. We got in the gate just in time. It was at our heels. Luckily, our local park was just over the road, and the dog heard other dogs barking and just took off over the road heading for the park. It was a lucky escape.

Shaila and I were left standing in someone's garden with four greyhounds, it was just as well the house owners weren't in. We quickly got out and ran back home with the dogs, watching out in case the big dog came back. It didn't, and we got home safely. I think it was a young dog the way it was bounding about all over the place, and I think it had escaped from a garden.

All in all, the boarding was a great wee business. I did it for five years, and every year I got busier and busier. I did such a good job; all my customers trusted me completely with their pooches, and the owners of the greyhounds never let anyone know what happened to Rosie, it stayed between me and them.

The last couple of years I had the business, some of my dogs died. The greyhounds, one after another, went within two years. They were all gone. It was one of the saddest times of my life giving it all up, but I had to because I wasn't getting any younger. I was also dog-walking during those five years, only on a small scale and Shaila helped me with the walks. But it was tiring; all I did was walk, walk, and walk some more.

I was still working full-time; I could do between 20,000 and 25,000 steps on one shift. Then I went home after a twelve-hour shift and took whatever dogs I had in the house for a walk. Some nights I wouldn't get to bed till about midnight, and that was from 5:30 in the morning, on the go for all those hours. How many people could do that, I wonder?

In March 2017, we decided to go to Vegas. Mum always wanted to go, so we started her bucket list with Vegas. Me, Shaila, Stuart, and Mum arranged to meet my sister Dory there. Shaila wasn't sure she would like it, but the rest of us were excited to have a new adventure somewhere we hadn't been before. We went and spent a fortune there. The place is amazing, we went for two weeks, but you really need double that to see everything. We booked the third floor in the Stratosphere Hotel. The doors of the lift opened, and all you could smell was grass, and I'm not talking about the type of grass that grows in fields!

It was very strong smelling, which meant it was bloody good gear. I had stopped smoking weed for nine months until that lift door opened, and then it was all up in the air again. I was dying for a joint, after smelling that sweet aroma. Along the corridor to our room, you could smell weed. I thought this must be the smoking floor. We got to the room, it was tiny for four people, and there was soon to be five when Dory joined us in a few days. The Stratosphere wasn't one of the best hotels, but it was okay. We explored other hotels; some of them were beautiful. Ours was a dive compared to them, but the beds were comfy, and there was a flat-screen TV as well. The next day, Stuart and I got on the computer to see what the rules are about cannabis in Vegas. There was a dispensary just over the road from us. They said they could give a prescription at the cost of 40 dollars, and then it was a fortune to buy it, so we decided to go down other routes on the computer, and we got a reply from a guy who was willing to sell us some of his homegrown. A couple of hours later, he arrived outside the hotel with a half-ounce. Oh, happy days, I couldn't believe it! I wasn't expecting this to happen, and better still, we were allowed to smoke it in the hotel. I shouldn't have touched it again, but the smell was too much. I couldn't have stayed there, smelling it and knowing the guests next door to me were smoking and getting high. It's like asking an alcoholic to sit in a pub without touching a drink, virtually impossible. I thought, fuck it, what happens in Vegas stays in Vegas.

We went to a couple of really good shows, but there was so much more that we didn't see and do. The next time I go, it will be with people who like to have a drink and a good time. We did go to the Grand Canyon, and it was amazing to see in real life. The colours were so beautiful, it really was amazing to see it in front of you. Our time in Vegas was good; we got to see some beautiful hotels. The two weeks went by quickly. Shaila and Dory didn't like Vegas much, but my mum and Stuart thought it was great. Next time I go, it will be for longer, and I will take much more money with me.

We got back home at the end of April, and it was time for me to get busy with the dog boarding again. Like I said, Shaila didn't like Vegas and she said she didn't feel like it had been a holiday going there, so she wanted to go to Kentucky, like we did every year. Even though the Vegas holiday cost a fortune, she still wanted to go there but I didn't want to go on another four flights there and back. We had just done six flights to Vegas.

In the end, she and Mum went over in the middle of July. I had to work down at the cattery while Shaila was away. This was the busiest time of year for the cattery. It was back-breaking in the summer, between all the bending up and down you had to do and the heat of the summer it really was exhausting. During the summer, it would take about four hours to do the lot and I couldn't do it for any longer than that. Ellie was fifteen years older than me,

She would say that she was knackered after doing the weekend when we were off, but actually she never did any work.

Ellie was one of those people who thought everyone was stupid apart from her. We would go in on a Monday morning and see exactly what she hadn't done. We knew if it wasn't done because there would be shit stuck to the floor in the kennels and loads of paper in their cages because she would just throw the shredded paper that we used for the floor in their kennels. She never picked any of the shit up because she knew one of us would be in on Monday morning to do it all but would swear blind that she was knackered because of all the work she had done. She bare-faced lied. It was so frustrating, and it annoyed us immensely, but what could we do? She was still our boss/friend/part of the family/sister. She was all those things, but she could also be a hateful, spiteful, bitch and then she could be really kind and considerate. She was the most complicated person I've ever known. She was very intelligent and very successful. She had taken a job in the cinema when she was 17. When she was 18, she took on another job, bringing in a full-time wage doing two part-time jobs. It wasn't long after she took the second job, she moved out of her parent's house and into a little flat in Edinburgh.

After a while, she didn't think she was earning enough money. She needed something else that paid a lot more money. She saw an advert for a stripper. Ellie was blonde and had a really good body when she was in her twenties. She thought, why not? She would give it a go. She told me that she was making double the amount she had been making with the two part-time jobs, so it was a no-brainer, she was going to stick with it until she got what she wanted. A few months went by and her sister lost her job and asked Ellie if any jobs were going in the pub she was working in. At that time, there wasn't, but Ellie said, "I'll try and get you a few hours." She racked her brain about how to get some work for her sister. It wasn't long before she came up with an idea that she was going to put to her boss.

She asked him if he would be interested in having two strippers on at the same time for no extra charge until the place got busier, and if it got busier, then she would be expecting her sister to be paid. Of course, the place got busier; two good-looking blondes were stripping down to their undies four times a week, but the boss wouldn't pay any more money, so they quit. It wasn't long before Ellie had an idea that she and her sister would get another stripping job in another pub. They not only got one pub but two to take them on. Before long, they were raking it in. Ellie was getting into the swing of things now - she was clever. She noticed that the entertainment business was thriving, but she needed to know more about it. She approached an entertainment company that organised all different types of acts to play in pubs and clubs. Ellie and Reenie had great personalities, they were very funny. We used to have a really good laugh at times. They arranged an interview time so they could meet and show them what kind of act they were doing and if it was good enough and suitable.

The interview went well, and he offered them a job with the company.

Ellie was really pleased because she knew this was an opportunity that could bring in a lot of dosh. She already had a plan, she was going to learn the ropes of how an entertainment business ran, and then she was going to open one up herself, with Reenie. They spent a couple of years there and saved as much as they could so they could start up. The time came when they were ready to go it alone into the big bad world of business. They rented an office and started the search for some acts. They got a couple of acts, one was a female singer, and the other a comedian and they did their turn as well. As time went on, she got twenty artists on her books. She finally reached her goals to become her own boss and make loads of money.

I think they had the business for about ten years and eventually gave it up and went their separate ways because they weren't getting on anymore and they were fed up with late nights and men, as it was a man's world in those days. It was very hard for women to get on in business. Women were deemed only good for housework and producing babies. Ellie didn't like either of those two things; she didn't like kids and hated housework. Ellie thought about what she could do next and she came up with dog breeding. She started by looking for suitable premises.

She knew that it would have to be outside Edinburgh, and that's how she ended up near us. She bought a cottage with a big space around the back. It was situated on a main road, but the house stood alone. She had no immediate neighbours, but she loved that because she wasn't very neighbourly, anyway. She wasn't the type of person who liked people in her house for any length of time. The only time she would tolerate people in the house was if they were there to buy a puppy. Then they could be there any length of time as long as they bought one. Ellie didn't sell to just anyone; she had to make sure they were going to look after it. They would just have to say the wrong thing, and she wouldn't give them one.

I actually don't like dog breeding. I think it's wrong that people purposely get female dogs pregnant so they can make money off them. Ellie didn't have a problem with it because she was making a fortune out of it. I think she had a nerve, making dogs have pups when she never even had one child herself. Neither she nor I could know what it was like to give birth.

We knew it was painful and horrible and it was for the dogs too. Ellie stuck to the rules most of the time and never overbred her dogs. She would only get them to produce the limit of pups and then retire them, at the right age. She never treated her dogs badly, they were always fed the right amount of food and were regularly cleaned. Ellie was doing everything right in that sense, but I still didn't agree with it but, I decided that people were going to do this anyway, regardless of what I or anyone else thought. So, I said I would do the job because I loved dogs and cats, and at least I knew that as long as I was there, they would be looked after well.

The cattery was still running well too. The first year was quite busy, and then year after year, she was full every summer, Easter, and Christmas. A cattery is mostly seasonal, but she had some cats throughout the year too. Between the two, she was making a fortune. By the time she was 55, her mortgage was paid off. Ellie loved making money; it was the one thing that made her happy, but it wasn't so good for the paupers who worked for her. That was the way it was between us—she was rich, and we were poor and it looked like it was going to stay that way. We were talking one night on the way to the cinema about the state of the country as usual and I said,

"If you're loaded in this country, you'll be okay, but if you're poor, tough luck."

She said, "If you're poor in this country, then that's the way you're going to stay."

I thought it was really insensitive to say such a thing, as me and my family were in that category. I don't know if she realised that her statement would hurt me.

However, Ellie's words really made me more determined to change things and made me think about a way to bring more money in, and that's when I had thought about the dog boarding. I knew it wouldn't make me rich, but it brought in a few hundred pounds a year to help me out. It was a start in the right direction. Between the money I had and Shaila's money, we wondered what the best thing to do with it was. We knew that we didn't want to stay in Britain, so we decided this might be the right time to go to the States and open up a business. At first, we thought about a fish and chip shop because they don't have fish and chip shops in Kentucky, but when we found out it was 20 grand for one fryer, we realised we didn't have that kind of money. Then we thought about house flipping or renovating. We really wanted to do that, but it is a risky business. You can lose everything on your first house if you come across hidden expenses. To do that successfully, you would need contingency money, so we couldn't do that. What were we going to do?

We needed something that wasn't too strenuous and physical as we were both getting older. We needed something easy to do that brought in a lot of money. The answer was staring us in the face. My sister Dory's son Adrian had a partner called Amy whose sister had a business called Laser Body Contouring. This is done with a machine that shoots laser beams down into the fat, breaks it up, and you just pee it out. She was making a fortune. She was doing so well that she'd had to open another shop. We had to look into this. We got some more info from Amy, and it sounded great. It wasn't going to be difficult to set up, and the biggest expense would be the machine, brand new with 12 paddles (the things that lay on top of the skin to shoot the lasers through). The more paddles you have, the more expensive the machine. A 40 grand one was out of reach. We didn't want to spend a fortune on the first one just in case the business didn't take off, so we went for a two-paddle machine that cost 10 grand.

When we decided to go for that business, Adrian and Amy said they would help us set it up. In the past, those two had not been entirely honest or reliable, so why would we trust them? Only God knows the answer to that one, but we did. We thought we would give them a chance to show they had changed and the offer of help was a genuine one. My sister Dory loves him because he is her son, but she hates what he has become. It really is all down to his very lazy girlfriend Amy. She has had two sets of twins by my nephew and a single child also. I'm surprised she could be bothered pushing them out. She said she doesn't do house cleaning, and her house is a tip, and I really do mean a tip. Her car is at least 3 inches thick with juice cans, papers, and God knows what else. We didn't go in her car if we could avoid it, but her kids had no choice. Not only do they have to climb over the rubbish in the car, but when they went into the house, it was the same in there. Is that the best you can do for your kids?

Adrian was just as bad. He'd leave it till he couldn't stand it any longer and then yell at her to get the cleaning done. She wouldn't do it, so he would end up doing it with a threat of leaving her the next time it happened, but he never went through with that. They're like two peas in a pod; they're as selfish as they come. No one is more important than they are, not even their kids, as we were to discover.

Shaila had been talking to them when she was in the USA in September 2017 and said they really sounded genuine and wanted to help us with it. I still had my doubts. They don't usually do anything for nothing and they're quite happy to receive payment if you ask them to do anything for you. If we go anywhere with them, then you're paying because apparently, they never have any money, ever. Any meals or places that cost to get in, they never pay. This is not a good track record for them, but we decided to give them one last chance to help us out after all we had done for them. We needed help with legal things that would be hard for us to do on our own because we weren't Americans.

Between the money I had and Shaila's got for the sale of her house when her horrible husband / Second Chance Partner, refused to sell her, his share of the house. She would still have her house if it wasn't for him being a horrible bastard, he was the one that had an affair then crawled back years later as a Lodger, she was stupid enough to let him step back into that house. Eventually they got together again thinking they could rekindle, but he was still a horrible bastard and inevitably it didn't work.

In all, 2017 wasn't a good year. We'd been to Vegas, and I'd ended up on weed again. Shaila and mum went back to the States in July for three weeks, and that was when mum broke her knee. They ended up having to stay until September, and I had the cattery five days a week, the borders to look after, and the dog walking to do as well. It was too much, but I had to get on with it. What choice did I have? I was knackered every day and cursing Shaila for wanting to go over. They finally got home, and Mum had to come and stay at ours for the first four weeks. Then she went back down to her flat where we thought she'd be okay. We got her a trolley to walk with, and she was fine with that. I went back to work, and Shaila went back to the cattery. Things were back to normal, until November 7th.

It started as just a normal Wednesday morning. I got up at about 8:30, had some breakfast while I watched the morning news. My phone rang. It was Shaila. I answered, and I could hear she was in distress. I couldn't make out what she was saying. I thought I heard, "Mum's not answering the door," and she was coming for me to go with her. By the sounds of it, this wasn't something good.

I ran to the toilet, put my coat on, grabbed my phone, and ran out the door. She drove up as I approached the gate. I got in the car, and Shaila was in a state. I asked what was wrong because I couldn't make out what she was saying. She said, "It's Ellie, I think she's dead."

I said, "Wait a minute, what makes you think that?"

"When she went down to the cattery at 9 o'clock, the place was still locked up, and that was unusual because in all the years we have worked there, you know, when you arrive, the padlock is off the gate, and the door is open."

This was very weird. I was beginning to think she was right as we approached the drive to the cattery. We were both shaking and trying to convince each other that it couldn't be that she was dead. She might have fallen over and couldn't get to the door or the phone. We were hoping it was going to be something like that. We got out of the car, and the place was still closed up. We banged on the window and knocked on the door to wake her up, but there was no noise coming from the house at all. No screaming, no shouting, no banging, nothing, and I think that's when we realised that it looked like our worst fears might be true.

Something serious had happened in there, and we had to get in. We had the front door key, but there was another door after that, and it was locked. We didn't have a key for that because it was always open for us in the mornings. It was a glass door, but you could only see into the hallway. She wasn't there. I got my phone out to call the police so they could break in, but at that point, a police van drove up, and the officer asked if we needed any help. We told him what we feared and he got on the radio right away asking for assistance. He took us down to his van as I was freezing. It was the first week in November, a cold day. I forgot to put shoes on and ran out with my flip-flops on. About 10 minutes later although it seemed longer, the police arrived. They had a crowbar with them and got the door open. They went in, and we were still shaking because I think we knew what they were going to come out and say.

Five minutes later they came out and confirmed our worst fears, Ellie had died in the night in her bed. We already knew that she was gone, but you always have that small hope that it'll be alright, but it wasn't. Ellie was really gone. We were in shock, this was totally unexpected. We had all been going to see the best Elvis impersonator the next day, and we were so looking forward to it.

The police were satisfied that there were no suspicious circumstances. They got a hold of her sister Reenie and asked her if it would be alright to let us feed and clean out the dogs and the one cat that was in. She said yes, of course and she would be there as soon as she could. She lived in Edinburgh a few miles away, but we knew her and knew she wouldn't be in any hurry. The police arranged for Ellie's body to be removed and told us to go and get a coffee, they would let us know when she was away. We told the police that we needed to feed the dogs first as it was noon already. They let us do that and then we went up the road. I put some shoes and warm clothes on, we only had Jilly the golden Labrador to walk that day, thankfully. We had a cup of coffee and then went up to take Jilly out. Jilly was a very intelligent dog. She knew there was something wrong with us. She wouldn't leave my side. She would normally be running about and chasing her ball, but we couldn't get her to do anything. She just wanted to stay with us. She did her business and we took her back home. The police phoned and said Ellie had been taken away and we could get access to the property. We got back to the house and went in and cleaned the dogs out crying tears of bewilderment. We just couldn't believe she was gone.

There was another dilemma. We knew Ellie had a black safety box with money and documents in it. The last 2 years of her life she kept telling us what she wanted to happen when she died, although mainly to Shaila because she was the one working there most of the time. I only went down when she was going to her dog shows and would go and stay there and look after the place several times throughout the years. If it wasn't for us, she wouldn't have gotten anywhere. She trusted us 100% with her livestock, her house, her business, and her death. She said many times over the 4-5 years before she died that she was going to change her will because she was fed up with humans and she was going to give it all away to charity. She would say especially that her sister Reenie wasn't to get anything as she was a selfish person and had never done anything for her. When their father died, her mother wasn't far behind, and Ellie and Reenie inherited the house. It needed some cosmetic work done, and Reenie took on the task of doing it. Ellie couldn't do it as she had animals to look after and a business to run, whereas Reenie only had a taxi to drive. So she did the flat up and then decided that she was going to sell the house without Ellie knowing and keep most of the money, but Ellie found out and stopped her. Ellie asked her,

"Why did you even think about doing that?" She was very angry, and Reenie replied,

"Because I was the one that did the work to do it up." She didn't. The workmen did it.

They did a good job too, it was really nicely done. After that Ellie didn't trust Reenie with anything. She didn't trust her before that happened but even more so now. She said Reenie would just waste any money she got from her so she wasn't to get any. When she spoke like that, we took it with a pinch of salt to begin with, but the more she said it, the more we realised she was serious. She would say, "Promise you'll do what I'm asking," and

we said, "yes, we'll do what we can if it happens."

We honestly thought that we would be dead before her because of all the smoking and the chips we eat, or we thought Reenie would go first because she was a couple of years older than Ellie and she smoked all her life, but unfortunately, Ellie went first which left us in a sticky situation. We had to make a decision. If we found the box and there was money in it, what the hell are we going to do?

Chapter Twelve
The Box 2017 / 2019

There's a story within a story about the black box. About a year or so before she died, I was staying at the cattery for the weekend, looking after the place while Ellie was at a dog show. I needed a pen to note something down, but there was none at her desk, so I started looking in the drawers in the hallway. Nothing in the top drawers or the middle ones, but the bottom drawer had a real jewel in it. There was an oriental-type box, it was silver and looked like something you would see in an Arabian film. It was a beautiful, shiny silver box. I opened it up and couldn't believe what was revealed. It was full of money, folded carefully. It wasn't lying flat; it looked like there were five twenties folded once and then stood on their sides in the box. I don't know how much was in there, but the money was stacked in hundreds side by side, and it was tight. She couldn't have fit any more in the box, and the box wasn't small. I reckon there could have been anything between 20 and 30 grand, easily maybe more. I'm not saying I wasn't tempted, but I didn't touch it.

I thought that is not a good place to leave that. I thought she was smarter than that. Now I thought I had better make sure it didn't get stolen, so all weekend I made sure the doors were locked when I wasn't in the house. For if it went missing, I suppose I would be a suspect. I always think in advance about things that could happen.

Shaila came down to pick me up, and I showed her it, and she couldn't believe it either. It was puzzling. Why was the money there? So much of it, but it wasn't our business, so we just put it to the back of our minds and got on with things.

A couple of weeks later, when I was down there again, I looked in the drawer, and the box was gone. I thought no more of it until Shaila came in one day with a black safety box and said Ellie asked me to keep this box for her. She said, "I'm not sure what's in it. Ellie said it was documents she didn't want Customs and Excise to see as they were investigating her for VAT evasion,"

I think we knew there was probably money in it. We didn't know what was in it at the end of the day. We pulled everything out from the front door cupboard, which goes way back and has a slant on the back wall, so it's quite hard to get to the back of it. We pulled it all out and stashed the box beside the back wall and then just piled all the stuff back in and added some more, so if anybody wanted to go in that cupboard, it would put them off. Stuart and Sharon were in the house also. We couldn't let anybody get to that box.

The box was in the cupboard for about two months until Ellie got the tax thing sorted out. She was lucky they were only asking for the money she owed, which was about £80,000. She was lucky they didn't charge her with tax evasion or fraud. Ellie was worried about it and kept saying she would never survive in jail and would rather be dead. She said she would kill all her dogs and then herself if she was sent to prison. Luckily, it never came to that. She settled her bill, and that was the end of it. What a relief it was for all of us. Then she asked for the box back, and Shaila took it back down to her. Two weeks later, she died. In the last year of her life, she seemed different. She was always stressed out about something or another, but the last year, she was worse. The Customs and Excise situation didn't help, as it put enormous stress on her. It was two men in their stupid intimidating uniforms, talking down to her. They made her worried about going to court and going to jail. That's what she was worried about, not the money she was going to have to pay. She was forgetting things much more and seemed muddled. I think things got on top of her at that time, but it all came good, and then she died. What the hell, life is so cruel at times.

So, we had to find the box before Reenie arrived. We knew she wouldn't rush over, so we had time to find it. I'm not sure what we were going to do with it, but we just didn't want her to get it. That's what Ellie wanted, and we promised her we would do our best for her. So, we started to search. Shaila and I went to the bedroom first, looked everywhere, but no sign of it. Veronica was keeping watch at the big double window at the front. We went to the small sitting room at the back where Ellie spent most of her time. Again, we looked everywhere and found nothing. Next, we went to the spare room and searched there. We looked everywhere but couldn't find it. We couldn't think where it could be, and time was running out. It had been an hour and a half since Reenie had been told about her sister dying. We were baffled about what she had done with it. It wasn't a small box; it was quite big. We stopped for a minute for a drink and a smoke to think. I took myself back to the spare room and realized there was a case in the cupboard that I didn't look in because it felt light and empty. We ran through to the room, got the case, and opened it. And guess what? The box was inside. We couldn't believe it. Of course, it was locked. We shook it, and there was something in it.

We needed to find the key, but time was against us. Rennie could arrive any moment, so we had to stash it somewhere. It had to be a place she wouldn't find, knowing she would search for anything that might contain money or valuables, especially the will. Inside the house was out of the question; there weren't many hiding spots for such a large black safe deposit box. We attempted the large plant pots out back, but they were too small. It had to be somewhere she wouldn't think to look—outside. We settled on a spot between the cattery building and the field fence, confident she wouldn't think to search there.

No sooner had we hidden the box and returned inside, Veronica shouted, "She's here!" Reenie arrived in her car with Pam, a friend we hadn't met before, but who, it turned out, had been friends with Reenie for years. I made them coffee, and we started discussing Ellie's death and what to do with the 17 dogs she had left behind. Shaila began explaining Ellie's wishes for the dogs—to find them new homes.

"I've already contacted some potential adopters," Reenie said - "As we spoke the potential adopters arrived gave their condolences and expressed their shock and disbelieve at what has happened, they chose their dogs and left they all seemed nice people, Ellie knew them as they were all in the dogy world so we were happy the dogs were going to good homes." Reenie and Pam left with a couple of black bags away with them. I don't know what was in them.

After everybody left we put the kettle on and retrieved the box. It was locked, so where was the key, we looked everywhere and found a good few keys but none fitted the box, we just thought what the hell, so we got a screwdriver and a hammer and busted it open, when we opened it, it was just her, passport, birth certificate and a letter saying what lawyer had her will. I'm glad there was no money in it because what would we have done with it.

I felt uneasy. Shaila insisted this wasn't what Ellie wanted. Reenie promptly declared herself the executor, assuming the role before even knowing Ellie's choice, though she would later be confirmed as the executor of her sister's will.

Driving home, we were quiet, all our thoughts on what had just happened. When we had gone to bed the night before, we never would have thought all this was going to happen the next day.

It was past midnight when we got back to the house. We checked the dogs were okay and locked up for the night. The night wasn't over for us yet because we still had to find a place for the documents at Ellie's. It had to be somewhere that she may have looked before but somehow missed. We tried a few places before we decided on one of the drawers at her desk. This was the perfect place because there was a lot of paperwork and bits and bobs. In the middle, there was some plastic stationery stuff. This was an ideal place to put the documents because they looked like they were stuck in between the paperwork and could have been missed. So, we left them there, knowing that Reenie would be back to find them.

We were shattered and deflated, we still couldn't believe she was gone. We seriously thought she'd outlive us but someone had decided it was her time. The hard reality is she was gone and wasn't coming back.

We bunked up in the small living room to try and sleep. Shaila decided to still go to work in the morning. She hardly slept a wink. Veronica and I slept a little bit. But even in sleep, you can still feel the pain of grief. Shaila got back from work around 9:15. We fed the animals and cleaned them out. We had our usual dog walks to do as well, so we'd be out for a few hours. That would give Reenie and her scrawny little pal time to look for the documents we had carefully placed in the side drawer of her desk.

After walking the dogs, we went home to freshen up and change our clothes. Life had changed now; we were without our friend, our sister, our safety net. We're going to miss her for sure, for many different reasons. We headed down to the cattery in the middle of the afternoon, and Reenie was there with her friend in tow. We had stayed down there for two nights. We said we'd stay for as long as it took to get homes for the dogs that were left. She said that would be great because she couldn't stay there. She offered me £300 as wages as I don't get any money when I'm off work.

We were expecting to be there at least a couple of weeks, if not more because there were still about eight dogs left to find homes for. On the fourth day, when we got back from walking the dogs, she was there, and she and her pal were loading the dogs into their cars.

I said, "What's going on?"

"I'm shutting the house down as it's going to take a few weeks to find out how Ellie came to die. She couldn't afford to give me any more money to cover my wages, so I'm taking the dogs up to the animal rescue place until they got re-homed"

She said, "So you can pack up your stuff and go home."

I was surprised to hear that toxicology was being done because Ellie didn't take drugs; she didn't even drink. It was obviously a load of lies so that Reenie could chuck us out. It was too much bother for her to do what her sister had asked. It was easier to close the place up and put the dogs in the pound the last place Ellie would have wanted them to end up.

I was planning on going back to work anyway but between me and Shaila, we would have been able to stay there and go to work as well until the dogs were homed. But Reenie clearly wanted us out. What could we do? We couldn't refuse. We had to leave and go home. It was heart-breaking leaving.

We went home, reluctantly, but were glad to get out of the house as it's quite eerie being there after someone's died. I kept thinking I would see her. We were scared to put the heating on in case she was watching. Everything was upside down now. It was near Christmas, we were deflated and sad, and still in shock. It's not every day someone you love and have known for a long time just dies. It's a hard pill to swallow.

About a week later, Reenie told us her will had been read out and Ellie had left her estate to the SSPCA, except that she had left Shaila £10,000 in her will, but it hadn't been officially read out yet, so we were to keep it under our hats. The same applied to a friend of hers from Ireland, whom she had fallen out with but made up with years later. There was a condition on this gift: both of them were to help find homes for her dogs. Reenie had already done that with most of them. There wasn't much left, only about five dogs. Reenie must have been fuming because she was left with nothing, as far as we know.

Someone else died two weeks after Ellie, on a Wednesday night, the same as her. That was Brad. The drinking and smoking finally caught up with him. So here I was once again, going to another funeral. No one dies for years, and then suddenly, two people that I loved dearly, the two people that had the most influence on me and helped me navigate my life after the hideous childhood I had.

It was hard to overcome the pain the grief was causing, but those two taught me if you get knocked down, you get up again, every time. If you don't, then you may never get up again. When you're told you have to be tough and overcome any difficulties in life, it's the only way to go. What else is there apart from lying down and dying? If Brad had followed his own advice, he'd still be alive today. Ellie did follow her own advice, and she was taken anyway. Between the two of them, they created me and what I am today. Before I met them, I was nothing, just someone with an empty head and no positive outlook on life. We had no direction from anybody, no interest in how we were going to go from a very negative and stressful childhood into adulthood. Shaila and I learned very little at primary school and even less at high school, so what chance did we have leaving school with no qualifications and no incentive to do anything?

Things do come up for people like me who didn't do well at school. We can't all be in top jobs that pay a fortune. Even if we all had the brains to do so, it's just not possible. But the top dogs just can't help themselves. They show prejudice and disrespect to the underdog. Think about this—no underdogs, no cleaning done, no food served, no streets cleaned, no buckets emptied, and many more jobs that the so-called dregs of society do. We are underpaid slaves, there to be ordered around, looked down on, and disrespected because of the jobs we do. We should not be made to feel like this. We all came from the same place; we're all human. We should all be treated equally and have equal opportunities. Why should I go on the cheapest holidays when others are on luxury ones?

I work extremely hard at work, looking after mostly ungrateful people that also like to treat us like slaves, usually constant for twelve hours with three half-hour breaks throughout the shift.

I can do between 22 and 25,000 steps a shift which is anything between nine and ten miles and we don't just walk we are exerting ourselves physically as well. I can hardly walk afterwards as my whole body will be aching, so tell me why should I get shit pay and go on cheap shit holidays? This is a festering problem all over the planet and it has to stop. I truly hate my job now, so I need to stop doing it.

Christmas was just round the corner but it meant even less than it normally did to us that year. I still walked the dogs for another year after Ellie passed, I use to go up by the cattery with the dogs, it was shut for months whilst it was up for sale. There were a few problems with it as well but eventually someone bought it and that was like a stab in the heart, knowing that we'd never be there again.

During all this, Shaila was having problems with her ex and the way he was trying to sell the house from under her - mmm where have we come across that kind of behaviour before? The house was to be sold and he was trying to get a bigger percentage of the sale, just another typical selfish greedy bastard.

The next day, Shaila said she decided to use some of her ten grand to take us to Amsterdam for a weekend. That was great news, just what we needed. So we went and had a good weekend. It was bittersweet. Mum and I had been there a few years ago in May, and it was good. This time, it was cold and wet, but we didn't care. It was Christmas time, all the lights were up, the German market was there. It was so nice being there at Christmas time. It was a great little escape.

Eventually the house was sold after a few months and Ellie got her money. We had to decide what we were going to do with all the money, we had about £80,000 between us. One thing we knew for sure was that we wanted to do something in the US. At first we thought about a fish and chip shop as that is something you won't find in America but then we realised it would cost too much for the friers and to rent a shop to put them in, so that was out. Then we thought about restoring houses and selling them on, but that would involve employing men to do the work so not a good option. We thought about a doggy day care centre, but we decided we'd be too old for that. So what was it to be? We had to find something to use the money for as it would just be wasted otherwise. After we had exhausted all those ideas, Adrian, Dory's son said "Why don't you do what Amy's sister is doing with the fat-busting machine?"

We had never heard of a fat-busting machine. The procedure is called laser body contouring where a machine that shoots lasers down into the fat deposits inside and melts the fat away. Amy's sister now has two shops carrying out these procedures, it worked and she'd had to open another shop because she'd got so busy. She was now loaded with a big house and a Porsche. She had been homeless and living in her car before that. She met a guy who helped her out and then became her husband, they built the business together and are now living happily ever after.

Chapter Thirteen
A New Career 2019

It sounded like a good business to open, this treatment was obviously popular, so we decided to do it. We were going into the beauty business, melting fat! We decided that Shaila would go over for 3 months with Mum and Veronica's daughter Sharon to get the ball rolling, but there was trouble brewing as Dory wasn't happy about Adrian's wife, Amy helping us get the business off the ground as she knew what she was really like. She was devious, greedy, selfish, and a shit mother to the five kids they had, but we didn't know all this. Mum, Shaila, and Sharon headed over to Kentucky in April to see what we could do to start up the business, but Dory wasn't happy at all because Shaila and Sharon were staying with Amy and Adrian and Mum was staying with Dory. She didn't want Amy involved in anything because she is a user and an abuser of anybody that has got anything that she hasn't. Adrian, her son, is exactly the same. In fact, they were made for each other. They are liars and cheats and I feel so sorry for their kids. Selfish people like them shouldn't have kids.

I'll give you an example. She worked for a giant parcel delivery service, in the warehouse. Her hours were 7-3 but she didn't pick her kids up from the after-school nursery until they're closing the doors at 6. So where did she go, you might wonder. Well, she either came home and went to bed or went shopping, we think. Whatever it was, she wouldn't go for those kids until closing time. By the time the kids got home they'd be pretty tired, but with enough energy to make more mess in the house while she sat down with a fag in her mouth and her phone in her hand as usual, ignoring the kids. Then she'd go make the kids something to eat. She made stuff like pizza, hot dogs, macaroni and a thing called salamander steak, which isn't actually a steak. It's made similar to a beef burger and cooked in gravy. This was quite nice and a bit healthier than the other three things they usually got. She even opened a can of peas and carrots to go with it and made some mash – no, don't get excited, it was always out of a pack. When she does anything, like making the kids food or bathing them, which was only on a Sunday, she'd have to have a fag in her mouth. Imagine cooking dinner with a fag in your mouth, but Amy thinks that's just fine and she can do whatever she wants because they're her kids and she gets away with it. But I'm telling you right now those kids were subject to neglect and nobody was doing anything.

Amy was terrible with what she fed them. She'd give them big bags of crisps to eat before their dinner and chocolate milk and then the kids wouldn't eat the crap she'd made for them because they'd eaten crap an hour before. Then they'd run themselves wild until whenever. They would be ushered up to bed, a quick wipe with the wipes, and then jammies on and a cup of chocolate milk each. They never went to bed quietly and they would play about the room before going to sleep. By midnight they would be asleep but not for long. Sometimes only 2 hours later one of them would get up and either wake the others up or they would go to their parents' room door. They had a lock on their door and locked it every night so the kids couldn't get in, so the kids just thumped on the door and kicked it until they answered. This went on every night. No one was getting any sleep, especially the kids. It was a ridiculous situation because the kids were running the house through the night with bad behaviour caused by their parents by giving them unsuitable food and drinks loaded with 'e' numbers. No wonder they were wired!

After being up most of the night they were dragged out of bed about 6 o'clock and again wiped down with wipes and the two younger twins had their nappies changed. And it was all left up there, dirty nappies, half-finished cups of chocolate milk, clothes everywhere, bed bugs everywhere. It was like being in some other world. Any person with half a brain would know that giving kids chocolate milk before bed and during the night is ridiculous. If kids are thirsty, they should only get water before bed and during the night.

Adrian worked weekends as well so he didn't see much of the kids. Amy reckoned she was 'off' at weekends and she might as well have not been there, she would just sit on her phone smoking all day and let the kids run riot about the house. She's a shit mother. I wouldn't want her for a mother or him for a father because they were and still are so selfish and unashamed of it. Anyway, they were living in a rented house that had no ceiling in the kitchen and Shaila and Sharon ended up sleeping on the couches in the half-decent living room. It was a square living room, quite big but it needed decorating and new furniture. This house had really high ceilings with a big whirly fan on it. They had a two-seater couch and a three-seater, and then in front of a big old fireplace was a double couch bed just with a metal frame and a mattress that folded into it when it was a couch and folded back out again when you wanted it as a bed. But of course, it was riddled with bedbugs. They said that they had tried to get rid of the bugs with bug bombs and stuff but they always came back.

This is because an impregnated female can lay one egg a day, seven a week, thirty a month, and each one can live up to four months. I think once you've got bed bugs, it's extremely hard to get rid of them. If you stayed with Amy and Adrian, you would encounter them eventually. While we were horrified at the thought of them crawling on us as we slept, Amy and Adrian seemed fine with it, and they seemed to be okay with them crawling over their kids as well. We weren't. It was bad enough that we had to put up with them, but to let the kids sleep with bugs is just totally wrong. Dory had the same problem, but she waged war on them and fought them with an alcohol solution that killed them and constantly washed covers, curtains, and things like that because that's where they liked to live. They like seams and hems to hide in. If you find one in your wardrobe, you really have to wash all the clothes in it and then put them out in the scorching hot sun for a few hours to make sure they're all dead, and even then, there could still be one there, hanging on. They're terrible things to have and very hard to completely get rid of. They say it's just one of those things that Americans have to learn to live with. There were also ants running about the sideboard next to the sink, on the other side of the sink, where the bin was, next to the back door. The bin was always full of everything, including food and nappies. It was disgusting, but once again, it didn't seem to bother them.

Shaila thought she had to do something, so she put the bins out and cleaned around the wall area and then cleaned behind the washing machine and around the sink area, to clear the area of ants. But the minute a bit of food was left on the counter or the bin was too full, the ants would be back. She didn't care; she just left food out and spillages on the counters and the floor, so the ants would congregate time and time again. Every time we cleaned up, she was behind us making a mess. I can tell you, this girl has no shame. Shaila cleaned the house every day, and Amy made sure that she and the kids messed it up again every day. It went on like that for the three months they were there. Shaila and Sharon came back at the beginning of July, and when the three of us went back in August to their house, it was a tip again. The ants were back and the bed bugs too. What an ignorant person, having people come to stay with the house like that. So once again, we had to clean it all up, not just for our sake but for the kids. She might like living in a pigsty, but why should the kids be forced to? It was a long, ongoing battle with this, and she wasn't looking after the kids right either. For instance, they were only bathed once a week on a Sunday, and the rest of the week, they were wiped down with wipes. It's disgusting and totally wrong.

The atmosphere was not good. As the weeks went by, Sharon, Shaila, and I ended up sleeping in the living room on the couches until Sharon started getting bitten by the bed bugs on the metal futon-type couch. She was getting eaten alive as they fed on her blood. We had to clean everything with bleach and an alcohol solution to kill any eggs and bugs we could see, but you'll never get them all. You need an exterminator. It's a long process and costly, so that was obviously not happening because they couldn't pay their rent or anything else on their $4000-a-month wages. They also get $500 food vouchers from the government as well.

They very rarely bought the kids anything new. Their clothes are either hand-me-downs or second-hand, free from the church. They're always pleading poverty, so where does all that money go? Because when we were over there, they were in debt with their rent. The electric board was after them for $850 that they owed for electricity, or they were going to cut it off. In fact, they told us it had been cut off, but it wasn't. Adrian went down to the basement and switched it off one morning so we couldn't use the air conditioning, the cooker, or anything else for that matter. Why? You might ask. Well, it was all because they wanted us to give them the money for the electric bill. They didn't ask, but they were dropping hints everywhere, and we heard them, but there was no way were we paying the bill, not after finding out the amount of money they were bringing in that should more than cover all their bills and still have money over. They were always skint, and we were now getting on their nerves by being there every day and not giving them anything. But of course, they had apparently forgotten that over the years, every time we went over, we always gave Adrian money. Every time we went somewhere, they had no money, so we would have to pay, or Dory would, and you'd never see a penny back from them. Like I say, they've no shame. This time around, when Shaila and Sharon went over first in April, Shaila had bought a TV for their living room, she bought a TV for Stuart's flat and other bits and pieces, and I ended up paying for a couch for his flat on my credit card that I've paid for since we came home. They also helped themselves to any shopping Shaila bought, like cans of juice, cereals, milk, anything that they liked, they just took. Amy was constantly shopping but not paying for any essential stuff. After a couple of days, we went out and when we came back, the air conditioning was on and the lights and the cooker were back on. We thought that's odd considering the electricity was cut off.

Someone had a lot of explaining to do. They came up with some cock and bull story that we misheard and they'd said that Adrian was taking out the electricity because they couldn't afford to use it as there were too many in the house. Of course, it was all an attempt to get us out of the house. He was only letting us use the lights and sockets. The fridge and freezer were still on. Imagine treating your family like that, what a pair of idiots.

This went on for about a week, then everything came to a head one day because Adrian said something about us not helping them out, but that's all we ever did was help him out and whatever scrag end he would be with at the time.

Before Shaila and Sharon left to come back to Britain, she gave them $500 for a car because their car had conked out and they needed one to take kids to school and nursery and for them to get to work. They both need a car and one car had to be at least a six-seater to get all the kids in as well as the driver. She usually had the bigger car because she picked the children up from school and nursery. No car was bought with this money. We still don't know what they spent it on, but that's them all over, doing what they like with other people's money. As usual, Shaila hadn't confronted them about it until now. They wanted us to pay their electric bill, which was $850. We said no chance and that was when Shaila said, "Do you want to tell us what happened to the $500 I gave you for a car that a so-called friend was selling to you? You obviously didn't buy a car because you don't have it and you don't have the money either, and now you want us to give you even more money for your electricity?"

There was bad feeling between Dory and Amy because when Adrian was in jail and she had nowhere to stay and was pregnant with their first set of twins, Dory let her stay with them. She also helped her out by paying for her car insurance. Amy was supposed to give her the money for it, but of course, she never did. There had been bad feelings about this for a few years now. This is what Adrian and Amy do, they get people to shell out money and then when something's said about it, they don't like it and there's a big bloody argument. This time was no different and there was a lot of shouting and screaming. I told Amy she was a sorry excuse for a woman. Adrian went roaring up the road on his motorbike like a bat out of hell. Dory was worried, of course, that he would kill himself. He came back about ten minutes later, intact.

He came into the house, and Amy told him that I'd said she was a sorry excuse for a woman and told him she wanted us to leave. I thought, what a fuckin' nerve they've got! We were going to leave anyway because of all the noise with the kids, all the stress and anxiety caused by my nephew and his cow, all the ants crawling about the counters over everything, and bed bugs crawling over you during the night. We were glad to leave the house of horrors but still, I couldn't help but cry as we drove away. I cried for the kids and the poor cat that was suffering terribly. We still had a month to go until our flight home, so we had to go over the bridge to Ohio to Stuart's flat. It was either that or renting a room in a hotel for a month, which would have cost a lot more than the month's rent for Stuart's flat. It was up the third floor and there was no lift, so that was painful for us but it was worth it to be away from Adrian and Amy.

Chapter Fourteen
Going Back Home 2019/21

We sent our paperwork on the 30th of October 2019 and we came home on the afternoon of the 31st, so we had to miss Halloween. As always, we said our goodbye to Dory since she was the only one there to see us off. The first flight was a nightmare as the turbulence was really bad; I seriously thought, "This is it, we're going down." Of course, we did not crash, but it really felt like it was going to. I wouldn't want to experience that again.

We touched down on British soil once again on the 1st of November 2019. It was cold as usual, our lift was late as usual, so nothing had changed. But something was coming that none of us would expect or want; it was coming to wreck our lives and disrupt humanity in a big way. Christmas was around the corner once again. Stuart decided to grow up a bit more and started to look for a partner. He went on dating sites and got a couple of dates, but the girls weren't for him. Then he met someone that was. Her name was Derry and her last name was the same as ours! What are the chances of that happening, two people that meet with the same surname? They seemed to hit it off right away. She liked fishing, which is Stuart's favourite pastime, and she supported the same football team as him. She smoked as well, she was literally his soulmate, and he was hers.

Christmas came and went. We thought that was going to be our last Christmas in Scotland, but it wasn't to be. We didn't know it but we were going to spend another two Christmases here. On the 31st of December 2019, it was announced that China was infested with a deadly virus that was attacking people's respiratory systems - people couldn't breathe. It was all over the news, reporting from China. The hospitals were getting overcrowded with people who couldn't breathe. It was terrible to watch. It was called COVID-19, a deadly virus that was wreaking havoc in China where it started, from a bat in a wet market, although there was also a strong theory and some scientific evidence that it could have possibly been man-made in a lab in China by two scientists.

This man and woman were delving into things that other scientists were very wary of approaching. They spoke openly in a documentary about it all. It didn't take long for them to realise how deadly it was, people were catching it and dying left, right and centre. I saw a poor Chinese man on the news just kneel over and die in the street. It was horrible to see, it brought it home how deadly and ruthless this virus was.

Everybody was in shock and disbelief that there was a deadly virus on its way to kill us. By the end of January, they were saying that the virus was out of control and people were being left to die. They were running out of oxygen and staff to treat the masses of people who were infected. Things weren't getting any better. By February, other countries were reporting people infected. It was spreading and spreading fast; they had to figure out a way of stopping it.

Populations were advised to keep their distance from anyone showing symptoms, which at that time meant showing signs of struggling to breathe. Other symptoms were discovered later on. The virus was spreading through human contact, handshaking, hugging, kissing, coughing and sneezing. The government made it clear that everyone was to wash their hands with soap and water frequently and to use sanitiser in between hand washing. This was good advice and it was the same advice all over the world. These sanitising practices were going to make a difference, but we wondered why they weren't mandating face covering. Didn't it make sense to cover up entries to the body that the virus was attacking? There was talk of face masks being worn, but initially, some idiot or idiots decided that it wouldn't be any good wearing face masks.

To me and my family, it was the thing we needed to do along with the other three precautions. By the beginning of March, there were reports of more deaths and thousands needing treatment, in other countries. It was coming our way and there was nothing we could do to stop it. I was still working, but I was so scared I was going to get it. Shaila and Mum have health conditions so they can't be put at risk. Because we all stayed in the same house, it was difficult to decide what to do. I was working in the hospital, and patients and their relatives could be bringing the virus in with them. By the sixth of March, I was getting really stressed out, crying before going in to work, shaking, and feeling dizzy. I didn't want to be in that environment where my life and my family's lives were at real risk. I was going to have to stop working. The last three shifts I did were on the 4th, 5th, and 9th of March 2020. On those shifts, I was going around all the door handles and keyboards, anything that was touched with hands and cleaning them with disinfectant. Nobody else was bothered that the virus could be on any of these things that were being constantly touched.

Visitors were still coming in and I thought, 'This is madness, they are probably bringing the virus in with them!' When we were talking about it, one of the nurses said, "What's all the fuss about? If you get it, you get it." What a ridiculous thing to say. That was on my last shift and it just convinced me that my decision to stop working was the right one. I didn't have much faith in the NHS or human beings, and my God was I proved right.

After that last shift, I went home, feeling relieved that I didn't have to go back there for a while. We decided to start wearing face masks everywhere we went. We were convinced that wearing a face mask would most definitely stop the virus from going into your mouth and into your nose. I think it was pretty obvious, but not many others had the sense to cover up at that time. We went to Tesco wearing them and people looked at us as if we had horns, but no, it was just a face mask to protect ourselves. I bet if they caught COVID, they would wish they'd had the sense to see that it made sense to cover up. We were well prepared, we wore our masks, cleaned and sanitised our hands, and stayed back from other people. We washed packaging anytime we went shopping and we cleaned anywhere hands touched, as I mentioned before. Doing all this meant none of us caught COVID.

The first two people in the UK who fell ill from the virus were reported on the 29th of January 2020 and many more were to follow. Everyone should have been wearing face masks at that time, but they weren't. I'm sure if face masks were made compulsory earlier, there would have been a lot fewer deaths. How come we figured that out and all the official brains who are running the country didn't? Still, to this day, I don't know why they left it so late. It would have been down to a pencil-pushing idiot in a suit, no doubt. Well, whoever you are, you caused a lot of misery and death. You should be sacked, and any other idiot that agreed with you should be too. Eventually, someone with a bit of common sense must have realised that wearing face masks would help the situation and it was announced that face coverings should be worn in all indoor public places. It was too late because a lot of people died, including medical staff. Some people got very ill with it but survived. Only after the face masks became mandatory did we see the deaths slowly reduce.

April came and went and the virus was spreading like wildfire throughout the world. Brazil was hit hard with it because their dickhead leader Jair Bolsonaro was telling the public that it was nothing more than a flu virus and that they should just go about their business as usual. The result was catastrophic - thousands of Brazilians died as a consequence. The same happened in India, it wasn't taken seriously enough at the start of the pandemic and there were a lot of lives lost through bad leadership and lies. Unfortunately, America was run by Donald Trump when the pandemic started. He is a first-class idiot. I don't think anybody could imagine how harmful he was. He mocked mask-wearing for a while, he refused to wear one and then he caught COVID. He didn't have it badly, but bad enough to start wearing a face mask thereafter. Trump caused nothing but hate and division in the States. He should never have been president in the first place. He was a businessman in the first place and had no authority over anyone except his employees, who he could get rid of at will, that's all he was. He wasn't a politician first then president, he knew nothing about running a country and he proved that. What was America thinking of? Didn't they already know he was an egotistical maniac, and like any other egotistical maniac, only them and theirs matter, no one else? At the time of writing, we are looking at another term with him in charge! Unbelievable!

By the time May arrived, things were looking really bad. A lot of the elderly were dying in care homes.

Many of them went to the hospital first for other ailments and then caught COVID and were sent back to the care homes without being tested for the virus. Of course, it spread like wildfire. Eventually, they realised that medical staff should wear personal protective equipment to protect themselves and the patients they were treating. Then it was decided that visitors were to cover up in hospitals and health centres. It extended to public transport and shops. The face coverings should have been implemented at the same time as the social distancing and hand washing. All you need to look at is how it was transmitted.

Fortunately for us, we didn't have anyone to be hugging and kissing, or carrying out any other risky behaviours and we weren't seeing other friends or family, so we were well protected in that sense. Also, we were wearing face masks long before the government decided it would be mandatory. It was discovered that COVID affected other organs as well, further down the line. Then, once you think you've recovered some people suffer from long COVID, which means even though they'd got rid of the infection, they would still have the after-effects.

Some had it worse than others. Our motto was don't catch COVID, and you won't risk any COVID problems. That worked for us. By the middle of March, a lockdown was announced. Everybody was to stay indoors as much as they could, shops were to close except essential shops like supermarkets, corner shops, takeaways, and garages. That was about it. Employers and the public were told they must work from home if they could and if they couldn't, they were to stay off work and go on a thing called a furlough scheme.

This scheme gave workers 80% of their wage paid from the government, and their jobs were kept safe. Nice for some people. Businesses had 50 grand awarded to them whether they needed it or not. Some of them were filling their pockets, while others, like me, got very little or nothing at all. I ended up spending the £1500 I had left in the bank over the four months I was off. It was good having the time off, but it was bittersweet because I wasn't getting paid.

I have zero contracted hours with the NHS. This is a terrible contract because you're not entitled to sick pay, even if you are diagnosed with cancer or your leg's hanging off. You get nothing. We only get half the holiday pay the permanent workers get, and it's not enough. We don't get enough time off. I have been doing this terrible job for 20 years, and that's the thanks I get. Everybody was told to stay in and stay away from everyone—including relatives, boyfriends and girlfriends. We were all to stop mixing because this is what was spreading the virus. That didn't bother us as we were all staying in the same house anyway, except for Veronica and the boys. When we went out with the dogs, it was like a ghost town. There was hardly a person to be seen or a car. The buses were running, but there was hardly a soul on them. We would count how many people were on the buses when they passed; it was around 2 or 3 per bus.

It was like something out of "The Walking Dead, A Zombie Apocalypse." It was eerie and scary. The government said that people were only allowed to go out for exercise once a day and were to limit trips to shops. The supermarkets had a queuing system and had to limit how many people were in the shop at one time. We didn't want to go more than once a week anyway. We hate shopping unless it's on holiday. It was worrying—what was going to happen to mankind as the virus caused havoc killing people? Then there was news that scientists were close to finding a vaccine. This was good news. After a few months, the vaccine was developed by two British female scientists, and another vaccine was developed by a British couple, also scientists. Without delay, they trialled them, and within a few months, vaccines were ready for an eager public. The very old got it first, then the disabled, then people with serious health problems, then the healthcare workers, and finally the rest of the public that were fit and healthy. Thank the Lord we found the vaccines because, without it, I think most of us would be dead by now. Definitely, the elderly and unfit would be. Mask-wearing, lockdown, and the vaccine were our saviour.

We were called for the vaccine and we had it gladly, but some idiots didn't want to have it. They were fools. Why would you not want to protect yourself against such a deadly virus? It didn't make sense. Those refusing vaccination included some of my family members who are also idiots. At Christmas 2020 lockdown rules were eased a bit from not being able to see family members that didn't live with you to being able to see them outside. It wasn't ideal, but we went up to Veronica's and had Christmas dinner. We put up a shelter, turned on a burner, and some lights, and had dinner outside. Luckily, it was warm that Christmas day. New Year came and went, and it was 2021. The virus was not as destructive as it was before the vaccine came. Deaths were going down and the number of people catching it was going down. It was really good to see the light at the end of the tunnel, although it was still in the distance.

The numbers of deaths and admissions were going down every week. People were slowly going back to work and schools, and most importantly, hairdressers. Everyone's hair was growing and there were no hairdressers to cut it. There were some funny hairstyles about.

The airports opened slowly. Some countries opened up with strict rules. You couldn't fly if you hadn't had the vaccine yet, and they wanted you to pay for COVID tests—one before you left, one when you got to the other foreign airport and the same coming back. That was four tests at about 80 euros a shot.

A lot of people couldn't wait to go away, so they paid for the testing. It wasn't a good idea because when people got to their destinations, they were only there a few days, and then they were told the virus had risen again and they had to come home within 48 hours. People were panicking, so there were masses of people turning up at airports trying to book flights home. People were going via other countries—it was pandemonium. Thank God we didn't go at that time. We waited until things had calmed down.

Because Mum had been diagnosed with dementia around July 2021, we wanted to take her to the States to see everyone, but that was not possible as America was still closed to the world. We waited until September when things were looking better. We started to look at Europe. Sharon was turning 18 on the 29th of September, so we were looking for that date, but they wanted everyone to have double vaccinations, and they had to have their second one 14 days before travelling. She would be four days out to fly on the 29th, so we had to make it later. So we decided to go on the 6th of October. We looked into it, but it still wasn't easy. You needed proof of vaccinations and you had to fill in a passenger locator form and another form relating to health. It didn't sound like a lot, but it wasn't easy. After a very stressful week, we managed to book a holiday to Malta for the 6th of October 2021. We had all the forms to fill in for me, Sheena, Sharon, and Mum. I started them, and it wasn't easy, but we got them done, and it said we needed to wait for a QR code to be sent to us. The weekend passed and still no code arrived. I started to panic and stress out. Tuesday night came—we were leaving in the morning at 7:30, and the code still hadn't appeared. I knew we weren't getting on that plane without it, so we went anyway, hoping it would sort itself out. We couldn't get the boarding passes done and we hadn't ordered our day 2 return COVID test that you've to do when you get home, so it just wasn't going well at all, what a disaster. We waited in the queue at the Ryan Air corner of the airport. They used to have a check-in desk with a person who could help you, but now it's a space with machines and weighing machines to weigh your baggage. There were two members of staff barking at people—nothing unusual for this airline. They're usually rude and unhelpful, and this time they were no different. We were getting closer to them. I was so tired and had already worked a 12-hour shift and only had 2 hours of sleep before we left. I felt like shit and just wanted to go back home, it was too much. We got to the check-in and had to tell the representative that the QR codes hadn't been sent to us yet. She didn't want to know; she just barked,

"If you don't have the right documents, you can't fly" and also, we hadn't checked in yet as we couldn't get it done. She just took the rope away and ushered us out of the line. We didn't have time for this. We went there 4 hours before departure, and it still wasn't enough time to get it sorted out. We were told if we didn't check in before a certain time, we would be charged £55 each to check-in. It was a lost cause; we had to accept that we weren't going on holiday, so we phoned a taxi and went home, absolutely exhausted. What a fucking disaster. But we had already decided not to let Ryanair defeat us, so we agreed we were going to do it all over again.

So back home we went, absolutely sickened and pissed off that once again money had been wasted and someone was once again benefiting from our misery. The next day, we went straight on the computer and booked the same holiday for the following Wednesday. We were determined to get Mum away and ourselves as we all needed a holiday.

It was just as nerve-racking as the first time, but we were sure we had it right this time. As we approached the front of the line, my heart started beating faster. Were we going to get through the gate this time? This time there was a nicer woman on; she was older and very helpful, and we managed to get through. Hallelujah, we were going on holiday! We got on the plane and took off, we were on our way. It was a good flight and a smooth landing. We got through customs, and then at the last gate, we still had a form to hand over to the Maltese authorities. Of course, there was something wrong. There were supposed to be two parts to the form, but we never noticed and only had page 1 of 2. Luckily, it wasn't a big problem as they had copies of the second form there, so we had to stand and fill it in, but we missed our transfer bus to the hotel, another problem.

Again, the girl at the desk was really kind, and she phoned the driver to come back for us. The transfer finally arrived, and the driver was an older man who talked and talked and talked. He just didn't draw a breath. He decided to go the country road rather than the mainstream roads as it was time for the school buses to come home. It seemed to take forever, and he wouldn't stop talking. Finally, we arrived at our hotel, which was facing right onto the sea and the pier. It was also facing the island of Gozo.

We were on the top floor, four flights up, opposite the sea. The wind was always there, and the sun never hit our veranda any time of the day, so it was always cold and windy and not an enjoyable experience when you sat out there. The day after we arrived, we realized the hotel was too far away from everything. There wasn't even a little grocery shop; there was a shop, but it was a gift shop. All we had was the hotel and a restaurant that was connected to it across the road, so that wasn't so good. Of course, we had to get a hotel that was at the back of beyond and had no sunshine upon it. What else could we expect?

We took off after breakfast to a little town called Bugibba. We had stayed there 10 years before. It had shops, restaurants, and a little bit of beach, but unfortunately, it was a day of thunder and torrential rain. We got some lunch, it was still raining. We did some grocery shopping, and yep, it was still raining. It just rained and rained, so we got the bus back to the hotel. We got dried off and decided to go down to the restaurant for some dinner. It was a nice place, clean and the staff were very good.

The day we arrived, we were late getting to the hotel apartment because of the stupid second page of the health forms. We had no milk, bread, water, or juice and nowhere to get it from, so we went down to the restaurant the first night for dinner. We explained what had happened, and they gave us some milk, coffee, and sugar, which was really kind of them, we left them a big tip.

The third day was nicer; sunnier and a bit warmer, so we decided to go to the little beach up the road. All the beaches are small in Malta, it's just little parts of the coastline that have some sandy bits and little spaces so you can walk into the sea. Most of it has seaweed and rocks in the way. Malta is very rocky and marble-like. It's quite a rugged, ancient place that's riddled with war landmarks, ancient caves, and crystal-clear waters.

Chapter Fifteen
The Blue Lagoon October 2022

We had visited a place called The Blue Lagoon the last time we were there and we wanted to go back because it is a special place. We booked a boat trip to the Blue Lagoon, and for an extra 12 euros each, we went in a speedboat around the island and into the caves. We managed to get Mum on the speedboat and it was great fun. I think she enjoyed it. I know I did!

It was busy at the Blue Lagoon as usual. It's really just a cove with clear blue water, and food and drink vans on the rocks. There are deck chairs placed all around the edge of the water and on the rocks. It is a suntrap. It was a great place with a beautiful piece of the sea to swim in. Everyone was there to enjoy themselves, it was a really good atmosphere. Sharon was having a great time just drinking whenever she could. They served pina coladas in a whole pineapple. They gouge out the inside of a pineapple, blend it with the rest of the ingredients, and then put it back in the pineapple to drink from. It was very tropical and lovely, so we had a few of them.

That was on the second to last day. We were planning on going to the town of Valletta to do some shopping, but we discovered we'd overspent the day before, so we thought there was no point walking around shops if we couldn't buy anything. Instead, we decided to go over to the pier to see what time the boats left for the Blue Lagoon and how much it would cost. It was 12 euros each for the boat, and they left every half hour, so we decided to spend the last day at the lagoon. Sharon was happy about that because she loved it there. It was a nice, relaxing day, and there were fewer people than usual. The last boat left at 5, so we went back then, packed our cases, and went to bed.

The next day, we got home late in the afternoon. It was cold as usual, and we had to wait nearly an hour for the taxi to turn up, as usual. Back in boring Britain, there was no sun, no happiness and a shit job. What can I say? I'm still living the dream, or should I say the nightmare. The next day was quite a nice morning. I did some housework, took the dogs out, and then went to the store. After dinner, I settled down to watch the soaps, and at about 8:30, I received a text from my bank asking me if I had tried to set up two separate payments from my bank accounts. I knew I hadn't, so I pressed no and it transferred me to my bank page where I typed in my ID and password, and then it told me it had been cancelled. I thought, "Good, I caught that in time." I carried on with my evening and thought no more of it.

The next morning, I got a call from my bank to discuss the fraud attempt on my accounts, but I couldn't believe what I was hearing. She said because I'd clicked on the link, it put me through to fraudsters who had stolen £2,000 from my accounts. She said that they would be investigating it and my cards had to be cancelled. Once again, money was taken from me and had gone to God knows where. I had to hope the bank would refund it for me, but later on that day, a male from the bank called and said a lot of rubbish, like it had been authorised by my fingerprint on an iPhone 9. I told him that I didn't own an iPhone 9 because mine was a 6, and I didn't authorize any payments. He told me that the phone call I got the next morning wasn't from the bank, so I asked, "Who was it then?" and he said, "It would have been the fraudsters."

I couldn't figure all this out. The fraudsters had sent me that text, stole my money, and then phoned me the next day to tell me my bank accounts had been fraudulently tampered with and that they would have to cancel my cards. I don't see the point of that phone call from the fraudsters, they had already stolen the money.

The weekend passed and I heard no more, so I decided to go to the bank and see if they could shed some light on what was happening. The girl at the bank said it was sent to the fraud squad and they were making a case. She gave me the number to phone them, which I did, and she told me that they had retrieved my money and found out it was done on an iPhone 9. My money was back in my accounts, thank God, because losing two grand that I've worked like a slave for would have caused me to go mad, I think.

I went back to work reluctantly. What else could I do? I needed to keep the money coming in, but I was so fed up with the job. I'll tell you what my shit job consists of.

I get up at 5 am, start at 7 am with a handover from the night staff. I serve breakfast, help several people get washed and dressed, make beds, take people back and forth to the toilet, take the tea trolley around, clean tables, and refill water jugs. Then we give lunch out and help anybody to eat if they need assistance. That's the first half of the 12-hour shift gone, only another 6 to go. Another 6 hours for the establishment to get as much out of you as they can. They want as much blood, sweat and tears as possible because they're paying you.

I would like to say that first of all, before money and anything else, we are all human and we need to eat, drink, and keep warm. We need all those three things to survive. We also need money to buy these things.

So the way it goes is, if you have a job that pays good money, you can have essential things in abundance. On the other hand, if you have a shit-paying job, which is often the hardest of jobs, you may not be able to afford all three essentials. If some of us are starving and cold, the ones that are warm and full don't really give a flying shit because most humans are selfish and only give a toss about themselves and their own.

When I'm on the bus at six in the morning, I think about what kind of day it will be. I already know the answer, it's going to be shit like all the other thousands of shifts I've done in the 20 years I've done this work. Going to work isn't something I want to do. I don't like it. I'll openly admit that I don't think I was born to work because I hate it so much. Don't get me wrong, I'm not scared of work and when I'm there, I work very hard. It's the people that make it hard. If you're working with lazy people, and there's a lot of them around - almost every shift I do, I encounter staff that think they're exempt from working hard.

As far as I know, my contract doesn't say I have to work with and put up with people who also don't want to be there, but are getting much more money than I am, so it's not so painful for them. I just wish people would be a bit kinder and think that the person they are choosing to be horrible to may be going through shit outside of work, whether it be domestic violence, financial issues, addictions, or ill health. Also, just because you're standing, walking and talking doesn't necessarily mean you're alright mentally or physically. We have to come into work looking happy, even if your world is falling apart or you've hidden pain like I have in my knees, back, wrists, and neck.

So the job is a pain just as I'm in pain, and yet I'm the one that does 75% of the work and end up doing over 20,000 steps a shift. Yes, I still walk out of there, but I'm in agony and not in a good place, mentally. On most shifts, we get used like paid slaves or pack donkeys where you just keep piling stuff on the donkey until it can't carry anymore, and soon it will buckle and collapse.

This job is confusing because on the surface, the nurses are all sweet and nice, well, some of them are. It chokes some staff to talk to you. They act as if they give a shit, but they don't. They don't care that half my body is hurting. All they want is to do as little as possible and have us do the rest.

To the public, remember this - these lazy individuals are looking after your relatives. They leave buzzers unanswered until one of us responds. A lot of the time it's for pain relief, which is what the nurses do, not us. So the patient has already waited an age to ask for the pain relief. Most of the nurses are in no hurry to get pain relief, something I've never understood because normally if people are asking for pain relief, they're in pain and need it as soon as possible.

I discovered early on that I was right in thinking that people wait too long for pain relief. One day, I was at work and a nurse who worked in the hospital came in with abdominal pain. She was throwing up and she was obviously in a lot of pain. She was getting a taste of her own medicine because she also had a long wait when she wanted pain relief. I could see she wasn't happy. Maybe she expected faster service than what she was getting.

A few weeks later, I was working in the ward where she had been admitted. In the staff room, she was recounting her ordeal to another nurse. She mentioned that after experiencing severe pain herself, she would no longer delay when someone asks for pain relief, she vowed to get it for any patient as soon as possible.

We are the ones who run after patients hour after hour. Do you know how hard it is to run around after humans, usually twelve of them, all ill and needy? Most of the time, we are left with a lot of physical work with patients, which is mentally exhausting as well. It's not fair, and it's not right. Something should be done about it, soon.

Also, my mum had Alzheimer's now. Am I supposed to come home and go through it all over again? She's not getting up through the night just now, which is good, but what if she turns night into day and day into night? What then? Am I expected to be up all night with my mother and then go in and do a 12-hour shift? I'm sorry, but that is too much, even for me. I'm in physical and mental pain, but I'm still expected to go to work and look as if I'm enjoying myself and that everything in my life is okay. This is the illusion created out of fear of losing your job and having your life destroyed.

While I'm complaining about the NHS, I would just like to say that by August 2022, COVID was almost gone, but the nursing staff were still being forced to wear face masks against our will under very hot, uncomfortable conditions during heat waves. There was no place to cool down, all the staff rooms were as hot as the wards, and outside was also hot during the summer. It was just too much. We're not robots, you idiots. We need the same as anybody else: heat when we're cold and cool when we're hot.

The summer was finally over and autumn had set in. Christmas was coming up, but we didn't feel very festive as our lives were falling apart. We just had a quiet one.

The festivities came and went. It was now 2022, another new year. What would this one bring? Joy, misery, happiness, sadness, suicidal thoughts? Well, the answer turned out to be all the above, minus the happiness and joy, because 2022 started with a very grave warning that energy companies were going to significantly increase the prices of gas and electricity. Just when things were getting back to normal after the COVID pandemic, they came out with this, saying we were going to have to pay about double the amount we already pay. Everybody thought that couldn't be right, but days went by, and they were still saying it was a fact. Then you realise, they are serious. OMG, they are serious. So the energy companies rake in billions of profit every year, including this year, and they want the poor to starve, freeze, go about in the dark and even that won't be enough misery. People will start to lose their homes, and then there will be thousands without a home and thousands of houses up for rent with nobody to stay in them because who can afford to rent or buy a house when the power companies are taking your rent and mortgage payments?

A few weeks later, it was announced that the price was going up again in November. WTF, this is well out of order! Most people who rent already struggle to get their rent and council tax together, and now the government is allowing the energy companies to charge an amount that is almost a second mortgage. I haven't mentioned the food prices also going up, as well as petrol and diesel. It seemed that we had a bunch of muppets running the country, empty heads, ignorant when it suited them. If we had level-thinking people running the country, they would see that there isn't a money tree in poor land, only misery and resentment. Poor people only have a few pounds left after everything is bought and paid for, so where do the government think they are going to get another £200-300 a month more for something that should be free? It should be free because it is a necessity for humans to survive, so is food and drink. Those are the three vital things humans need, but they're going to be withheld from the poor.

The government know the facts but still chooses to ignore them. Everybody knows that they know the facts, and that's what makes it worse. It's the total disregard for people's lives and their children's lives. They have no problem with the elderly becoming ill and going into the hospital or the young being malnourished and suffering other illnesses. Of course, the government is not listening to the hundred or more doctors and consultants writing to them saying that this is going to undoubtedly cause massive problems in the health service.

Boris Johnson is no longer prime minister. He's been voted out, thank God. He just ran amok along with his Tory pals during COVID. They were enjoying themselves while there was a serious pandemic going on. The public were living with fear, anxiety, uncertainty and death, and the government was just doing whatever they wanted. One of them knew she had COVID but still took a train from England to Scotland and back. She was prosecuted for breaking the law because the law made by the Tories was 'no travelling out of your own area'. Another one was filmed being unfaithful to his wife by kissing his secretary. Again, the rule was no shaking hands, hugging, or kissing, you idiot. He had to resign.

They had to look for a new prime minister to continue making a mess of this country. There were a lot of them putting themselves forward for the job, most of whom were disregarded until there were six, then four, and then two.

I do not have any faith in our government. They are mostly from wealthy families, and I think now we can see the extent to which these greedy, horrible, selfish people are prepared to go, as in hoarding millions in their bank accounts and in their big expensive houses. The discontent and disregard for the poor run in their veins and their kids' veins, so it's an ongoing situation for Great Britain and the rest of the world. It doesn't work, having extremely happy people at the top where life is good and they have no worries. Then down the bottom are the extremely angry, hardworking, low-paid workers whose wages barely cover everything, even though they go out and work harder than people who sit on their arses all day and eat expensive food. A lot of them will go home to a cold house and beans on toast for dinner.

This divide doesn't work, it never has. You're born whether you want it or not. Some people think they must have kids. Some women fall pregnant unplanned and either get rid of it or think,

'Oh well, I wasn't planning on falling pregnant, but I'll just have it anyway,' so those kids are already unwanted. I used to know someone who had her kids so she didn't have to go to work anymore. I think she probably isn't the only one who has done that. So excuse me if I think some people have kids for selfish reasons. They're not necessarily doing it for the kids they pop out every second year. For whatever reason, there should only be one reason to bear a child, and that's out of love. You need thousands of pounds to keep them. All children need food, water, and warmth. These three main things are going to be in very short supply soon because the price of EVERYTHING is soaring. Soon they'll be so high they will disappear into the clouds. If you grow up in a poor family, you're more likely to stay that way because money talks and money rules. There's not much more important than money, so if you're born into a rich family, you're more than likely to be well off as an adult. So the circle keeps turning: the rich get richer, and the poor get poorer.

I would like to make a suggestion: how about giving people who work low-paid jobs a lot more money, enough money so they can pay bills and still have money for leisure and at least one holiday a year? The world would be a much better place. How would we pay for it? It would come from the rich because their tax would be higher and therefore paid into the poor's income. That's unfair, you might think. It's not really because the rich will still be doing the job they love so much and still be getting paid more money than the poor, and the poor will still be doing the jobs they hate but will at least be getting a decent living and life from it.

Every single person should be entitled to a good, happy life while we are here. It shouldn't be a case of a small number of people hoarding a massive amount of money in their several bank accounts, while the majority of the public have very little in their bank accounts or nothing at all. I think the poor are realising now just how much the government and their rich followers are prepared to go with this.

They're prepared to sit back and watch thousands of people starve because the energy companies are taking all their money to give to the fat cat shareholders who clearly don't care about the fact that, in the twentieth century, children and their parents are going to have very little to eat, be very cold in their homes and will be very angry and miserable. No food or heat for the poor, two of the three things humans need to survive. The third thing is water, that we had plenty of once the extremely hot summer was over. It wouldn't surprise me if some people only have water for breakfast, lunch, and dinner from time to time.

At the beginning of September 2022 the warnings about the cost of living seemed to be falling on deaf ears because the government wasn't doing much. They gave out £300 to the neediest like pensioners and the unemployed. The rest of us, including the rich, got £400 in six instalments over the winter. I don't understand why people who have more than enough money to pay these rates are getting anything. If you're sitting with a few thousand quid in your bank account, then you can afford it. You may not like paying that amount, but it's not going to break your bank or probably stop you from going on holiday next year either, whereas the poor who have a little bit of money put by, which they have no doubt worked very hard for, will lose any money they have saved. This will be soul-destroying for many.

I didn't know if many people would be able to cope with this. I think people were still mentally and financially recovering from COVID. I was sure there would be a tsunami of despair, worry, stress and depression coming and that it would cause civil unrest. What did the government suppose people were going to do when their kids were hungry and cold and when they went out and robbed the rich of anything they could get. I know this already happened, but I was sure that year would be tenfold with robberies and shoplifting. It would be years before they got through all the court cases for shoplifting and house robberies. Most of them go unsolved with no prosecutions, anyway. We were hearing reports that more people are having mental health issues, and the ones that had issues before are getting worse because of the situation. Domestic violence has risen or gotten worse in many cases, very sad to hear.

I don't think the government had thought about all these things. I think they must not have had a clue how deep the deprivation will feel for the people who already have nothing and the people who have very little and will end up with nothing. How bleak that future must seem, having to save a little money every month for years from the little drop of money you grudgingly get paid by your employer, who would love to have you work for nothing, most of them anyway. What about the suicide rate? They reckoned it was going to soar as well. So there would be more suicide patients and more self-harm patients on top of all the old folk coming in with pneumonia and other things caused by being cold and not eating properly. We expected to see some people making up things to come in as they knew they would be warm and fed in the hospital. Those were my predictions. I hoped I was wrong and things didn't go that way. But what other way could it go if people were cold and hungry? What did the government suppose people were going to do, sit and allow their kids to starve and their parents go cold that winter? I don't think so somehow. The British public might be a bit soft and slow on the uptake, but we are human with human needs that we have to live, and without them, many die. It's a simple case of needs must, and you won't stop a lot of people from taking and doing what they need to do to survive.

During the wars, there was a shortage of food because there was a war on and everybody was in the same boat, near enough. But this was a different situation. This war is between the good and the bad, the rich and the poor, fairness and unfairness. What century are we living in? We consider ourselves as the superior beings on this planet, but are we? I don't think so. We've goddamn near destroyed the planet, and we still think it's okay to have people starving while we throw food out in many ways, every day. For instance, even before that crisis, people were using food banks—the unemployed, those with low incomes. It looks like they will be using them more frequently now. Because everyone is being hit by this, the poor people who were slightly better off before, the folk who provided the food for the banks, can't be as generous now either. That means there's less free food, and any out-of-date food still gets thrown away from food shops. What kind of society would do this? How can anyone justify that? We seem to be going backward in time when folk were cold and hungry. Years on, not much has changed, which says to me we must change the way we govern and the way we look after some and not others.

Great Britain is known to be a civilised nation, but are we? Some of us are prepared to sit back and watch others starve and freeze. I'm slowly coming to hate this country and some of the people in it. The people who are in charge of anything—all professions, humans, animals, countries—need to do the opposite of what has been done in the past. We need to start understanding that it's not okay to treat the backbone of the ant colony with disregard. Without the soldiers working so hard, there would be no colony; there would be no queen. That's the value of the working ants. So come on, in the twentieth century, we need to be more respectful of this and start treating workers better. See them as just another human being doing his/her job, whether it be a cleaner or a top executive. Don't treat people with disrespect because there is often more to the person than the job.

Stop this massive divide between rich and poor; it's pretty ridiculous that it's still going on. You can see from history, as far back as the slave trade, that things have come far, but not far enough. There are still slaves, the only difference is they get paid now.

Chapter Sixteen
The Queen Dies 08/09/22

OMG, the Queen died. It was hard to believe. I remember I was sitting and getting my braids put in by the lovely Maureen and her friend Lorraine. We were about three hours in (it takes about five hours.) When it was announced on my phone that Her Majesty had died. I could not believe it, she had been shaking hands with Liz Truss, the new Prime Minister, only two days before. The public were told it was natural causes, maybe it was, if it wasn't, we'll never know.

Prince Charles would now be King of Great Britain. Who knew that all this would happen within just a matter of days? I'm not a royalist, but you have to give some respect to them as the monarchy makes this country special. Most countries in the world don't have a king or queen, but most of them love the idea of having a monarchy. The reason our Queen was so popular is she got out and about, she visited many countries in her 70-year reign. The royals are known for their charity work and fundraising, they don't just sit around all day on their thrones and do nothing. Prince Charles set up the Prince's Trust to help underprivileged kids and that's done a lot of good over the years. He has his hand in other charities as well. Princess Anne has done a lot of charity work as well, they all do what they can when they can, except for Andrew who had been partying with young girls by the looks of things, we hope he's learned from his mistakes. There are other Kings and Queens around the world, but they very rarely venture out of their countries. You never hear of any of the royals doing anything except ours, this is why a lot of the world is in mourning for our Queen. She was the one person people could rely on to be the same person. The word constant has been coming up a lot because she was, for 70 years.

She was at her favourite residence in Scotland at Balmoral when she passed away. All her family were summoned to her bedside earlier that day. They all made it on time except for Harry, he was too far away at the time and couldn't get there before she died, what a shame, he must have been so disappointed.

Before the Queen died, all that had been in the news, for weeks, was the cost-of-living crisis. Before that, it was the Ukrainian war and before that, it was COVID. Now it was the Queen's death. Day one, 8th September, it was announced late afternoon that she had passed, and so it began. The Nation was in shock; I think a lot of people, including myself, when we saw the photo of her shaking hands with the new Prime Minister, you could see she looked very thin, but apart from that, she didn't seem that ill, she just seemed to die all of a sudden which creates shock waves throughout the country; it's a lot to take in you can't believe it at first, but then you have to because it was really true, she did die.

Her Majesty died in Scotland, at Balmoral, on the 8th of September 2022; on the morning of that day, the news had not broken yet. The Sun newspaper had a front-page picture of Kate and William with their kids, George, Charlotte and Louis. They were reporting that it was the children's first day back at school and this time Louis would join his older brother and sister. The photo showed the five of them hand in hand walking together to the school all smiling and happy. They didn't know their world was going to be turned upside down just a few hours later.

By late afternoon, there was an announcement on the TV that all the royals had been summoned to the Queen's bedside as she was very ill and they all immediately stopped what they were doing and went. Harry didn't quite make it on time to see her and make his peace with her before she passed, he was too far away. Sunday 11th September, everything was already put in place to move the Queen's coffin from Balmoral to Holyrood Palace, a 175-mile journey that would normally take about 3 hours but took 6 hours as every time they went through a town or a city, there were crowds of people and the vehicles would slow down to walking pace so that people could pay their respects. The cortege arrived at Holyrood at 4:22 pm to be precise. The crowds were quiet and sombre, throwing flowers down to the road for her.

At Holyrood Palace, the coffin was then mounted onto the eight pallbearers' shoulders for a slow walk up the Royal Mile to St Giles Cathedral where Her Majesty's coffin would be until Tuesday when she will be moved from Edinburgh to London on an RAF jet. Charles, Anne, Edward and Andrew were waiting at Holyrood to start the walk behind their mother's coffin to St Giles. Both sides of the Royal Mile were full of people, quiet people videoing the event on their phones, videoing a major piece of history that they would remember for the rest of their lives as we all would.

The public queue was already forming, waiting to pass through the hall of St Giles to pay respects to the Queen and the new King. They took her into the cathedral, and the four grown children of the Queen followed behind, and when the coffin was laid on the podium, Charles stood at the head of it and the other three took their place on the other three sides to create a protective vigil for 15 minutes with their heads bowed. After the 15 minutes was up, they slowly left the vigil and four other guards took their place. The people kept coming all through the night, through the next day and the next night and then the final day to visit was Tuesday as they were flying the Queen to England on Wednesday. Luckily it wasn't too cold through the night, but people weren't bothered anyway, all they wanted to do was to pass through the cathedral for two minutes and pay their respects. It was really turning into an event, so many people, so many police and security, it had all apparently been rehearsed for years and you could tell it was, it was flawless right the way through to her funeral.

It wasn't nice weather in Scotland when the Queen died. When I left Maureen's house after five hours of getting my hair done, it was raining and windy, not too cold but it was a bit miserable. The next day, however, was glorious sunshine and the sun kept on shining right through to the Queen's funeral. It shone on all the processions and rainbows popped up during the week as well, although there was no rain. People were reporting and filming them as well.

Wednesday 14th September, the Queen left Scotland for the last time for her coffin to lie in state for another vigil in London before she was laid to rest. She arrived in London without a hitch and was then taken to Buckingham Palace where she was to lie in state once more for four days. Once again the public could go and pay their respects. Our new King and his siblings held another vigil at the hall. Charles asked the eight grandchildren to hold their vigil on Saturday the 17th of September, allowing Harry to wear his military uniform for that event.

On Saturday, they stood around their grandmother's coffin with heads bowed for 15 minutes. Fifteen minutes doesn't seem a long time, but I think performing the vigil in full view of the world and dealing with grief and pain, it must have seemed like an age. They all did so well and didn't cry, even although I am sure they wanted to. They had to keep a straight face, when all they really wanted to do is curl up and fall to pieces like we all would do.

Just like in Scotland, there were queues round the clock for the four days. People flew in from around the world, feeling they had to be there, or wanted to be part of the history this event would become. The weekend passed, and Monday arrived, the day of Her Majesty's final journey and her funeral. The last walk from Buckingham Palace to Westminster Hall. The sun was still shining on Monday, the 19th of September, and the crowds were there in their masses to watch. Big screens were put up in parks all over the country, and it was announced that the day was to be a public holiday. At 11 o'clock, the funeral began. There were 2,500 police deployed, the army, the navy and various other groups of military and guards. There was no way anybody was going to cause a terrorist attack at this funeral. I have a theory that inside the royal family, they knew she was on her way out long before but didn't tell because it would give terrorists time to put into action a plan to carry out an attack, after all this would have been a glorious event for any terrorist group to disrupt. Even if any terror group thought they had a plan for this special event, they didn't stand a chance of carrying it out.

Before the service, a tenor bell was tolled every 60 seconds for 96 minutes—the number of years the Queen had lived. The coffin was placed on a gun carriage pulled by Navy sailors from Westminster Hall to Westminster Abbey's West Gate, led by King Charles and Queen Consort Camilla. A bearer party was waiting to carry the coffin into the Abbey. It was a massive service with 2,000 people inside, including 200 key workers and volunteers, heads of state, and foreign royals, along with the huge crowds outside. It truly was a sight to see, and the sun was still shining through. They had a beautiful choir and altar boys singing the hymns, and it felt like heaven.

It was beautiful, and at the end of the ceremony, they had a lone piper on the balcony play a lament and then turn and walk slowly away, fading into the background. That was when I broke down. The pipes are so haunting and sad, they remind me of my sister in the States because she loves the pipers. Even as I write this now, I have tears streaming down my face because it was so sad.

The funeral was coming to an end. The Queen's coffin slowly lowered down to the vault where 11 other Kings and Queens are resting. She's now with her husband Philip, who she loved very much, her mother and father and her sister Margaret.

What now and what's next? Covid's been and nearly gone, the oil companies are allowed to keep their massive profits, and the poor are officially set to starve and freeze, and then the Queen's death. Now that's over, we have to go back to the cost-of-living crisis. The new Prime Minister, Liz Truss and the Chancellor decided to help the crisis by removing caps on rich people's bonuses, bankers, etc. They thought it was a really good idea to reduce the tax rate for the rich from 45% to 40%. I really can't believe I'm writing this; it's ridiculous, but it's true. They said it would give foreign investors an incentive to invest in this country. It was a big gamble for the government to take because if it didn't work, it could be catastrophic for the country. The exchange rate for the pound against the dollar was very low and needed to rise again, and they thought this was the way to do it.

This was NOT going to help the elderly and the people who were on benefits; they needed HELP then, not in two years' time. It was just another Tory racket for the rich. I suspect the last thing this country needed was this. So the country's going to fail. I can't see anything good coming in the future. When it's cold and miserable in normal circumstances, the British public are miserable. I don't know if putting misery on top of misery is a good idea. I think the British public is near the end of their tether, the end of the line, because the government has crossed a line that may have serious consequences.

What now for us? We don't have enough money to do anything substantial; we can't go to the States now or Spain to live. We can't access our money from the business account in the States because the value of the pound is extremely low. It's never been like this before; when we started going to America, we would get $2 or more to the pound. On the 14th of October 2022, it was $1.13 to the pound and only 1.11 euros to the pound. When the euro was first established, the rate was over two euros to the pound. As you can see, there's a massive difference in the rates. How can this be? The Chancellor was sacked after only three weeks in his job. Now someone needed to sack Liz Truss.

We decided that all the nonsense was too much, so we decided to go back to Benidorm with Mum to escape the misery of Britain. We arrived in Benidorm once again and our hotel was a step up from the 2-star ones we always seem to end up with. It was a lovely hotel right on the beach; we could even get British channels on the TV.

Chapter Seventeen
The Last Holiday 2022/23

For all we know, this could be our last holiday abroad for a while. As the dementia progressed, Mum was only going to get worse. I didn't know how we would cope. I still had to go out to work, and Shaila's still ill several days throughout the month and she's only going to get worse. I can't believe the two people I love the most are fading away while other people I love don't seem to give a damn about our situation. The love for them is disappearing from my heart; I hate to say that, but it's true. Cameron is in the States living his best life, but at least he came over to see us and spent some time with Mum and understands how hard it is for us. There's not much he can do living there, but he promises to keep in touch more often. Unlike Dory, she hasn't made any attempt to come over and see us or her dying mother; I think she is too busy doing nothing.

After all Mum has done for Dory—she went over for about four years to babysit her kids after school because they were working. Mum paid for her flights every time even though they were the ones asking her to go over; there was never an offer to pay from them. Then after Dory had an accident at work and hurt herself and after years of fighting for compensation, she got £47,000 for it. She came over a few months later to Britain to get free dental treatment; she does like a freebie to herself even though she had just got thousands. She got her dental treatment done in Britain because Britain didn't know they emigrated to the States years ago. She got thousands of pounds worth of treatment done because she had a few teeth missing and has had for years now. She always had bad teeth and gums, and it didn't help when she knocked both her front teeth out vaulting over a gate when she was a teenager, as she ended up with two false front teeth on a plate.

She'll avoid paying for almost anything; even now when she has a lot of money, She gets clothes and shoes from the church charity for her husband; she said he just wastes his clothes, so he only deserves free second-hand clothes.

She brought us a piece of jewellery from the Indian reservation before she came over; it was a necklace with a double heart attached to a thin chain. I think they were gold, but I've never seen a flimsier piece of jewellery it was probably worth $20. When I sold my flat, I sent her £500 as a gift to help her out as she didn't have any money because she had paid off her debt with some of the money and blown the rest or kept it. All I do know is all we got was a shitty necklace and a meal out!

It was our last day in Benidorm unfortunately, we never wanted to go home, but this time was different. Britain was in such a mess, who would want to go back? I'd been watching the news the whole time. The story so far was that Liz Truss had finally done the right thing and resigned. Boris had cut his Caribbean trip short to come home and enter the race to become prime minister again. He was up against Rishi Sunak and Penny Mordaunt, the two people who had been up against Liz Truss when she won. So we had a prime minister who was forced out and two people not deemed good enough for the position a few weeks ago who apparently now are. You really couldn't make it up.

There had been no campaign run for them, it was all done behind closed doors. Boris pulled out two days after coming home from his expensive Caribbean trip, saying he had 102 votes from the cabinet's politicians but felt it wasn't enough support so he stepped down. So the competition was between Rishi Sunak a multi-millionaire and Penny Mordant - just your ordinary politician, although I was fairly certain she could afford to pay her bills comfortably, throughout this crisis. No one knows much about her unless you're a Tory. It was announced on 24th October 2022 that the millionaire Rishi Sunak would be prime minister. I didn't know if it's a good idea to put a millionaire in charge who'd just had a new swimming pool installed in his massive back garden whilst the poor starved and froze.

This is what we are going back to; if we could've stayed we would've, but Brexit spoiled that.

Our holiday was okay. We didn't do much as we were restricted with Mum to what we could do as her mobility was getting worse every week. I realised that most probably, her walking was going to go first. She fell in one of the shops we were in, holding on to a clothing rail to step down from the shop onto the pavement and of course the rail fell and she ended up on the ground with the rail on top of her. She landed on her bum as usual but cut her finger. It was okay, I put a plaster on it and bandaged it up.

The holiday was almost over, It felt like shit to go home to messy Britain, but we had to. The thought of going back to my shit job didn't fill me with joy, rather with dread. My knees are killing me in bed at night and I can hardly sleep, they're sore through the day also now and yet I'm supposed to still be able to do 20-23,000 steps a shift. I'm someone in pain that has to look after several people in pain and other illnesses at work and put up with all the bullshit from them also. The aircraft took off on time and we landed on time, it was 23:50. We were so tired. Stuart was waiting for us outside. It's a long time from leaving the hotel at 11 o'clock in the morning until almost midnight on the same day. It still amazes me that you can be in one country the first half of the day and in another the second half of the same day.

So that's us done it again, we went to a foreign country and managed to get back in one piece. I don't know if we'll go flying again, it's too much like hard work, maybe we'll go holidaying in England for a change.

We were back home, it was depressing, cold and dull, and the fact that the Tories were still running the country was even more depressing.

So the new extremely rich British/Indian Rishi Sunak took the next two weeks to try and come up with a better plan than his 47-day predecessor Liz Truss. He said he would address the nation on the 17th of November to tell us what he has come up with. I thought it would be in his best interest to grab the oil companies or whoever it is that is responsible for this cost-of-living disaster by the balls and don't let go until they were prepared to do the right thing and give up their profits and stop robbing the poor of every last penny they have.

One of the big giants revealed that they'd made double the amount of profit they'd made last year at the same time. It was truly disgusting and despicable to see how they could watch most of the country suffer like that. How did they live with themselves or sleep at night knowing that they are partly responsible for kids going hungry and cold, people having to give up their pets, their houses, their relationships, the hope of a better life, all because of the greedy bastards that want it all to themselves? Why does anybody need millions sitting in their bank accounts? The answer is they don't need it, it's mostly about power with these people.

For example, why can't the richest man on earth, apparently Elon Musk, give half of his zillions to the poor, he would still have more than enough to hoard, and even better than that, why can't the rest of those who are hoarding millions and billions do the same and help the world, the people that are starving, the animals that are dying, the killing of the planet that you have helped to destroy. Remember this, all your millions won't help your children and nothing's going to help your grandchildren survive what they are going to be facing, money won't save them, it will be useless.

So the planet will be destroyed through greed and the self-indulgence of humans, whoever invented us shouldn't have bothered, it should have just been animals and insects and of course sea life. The planet would look so different if humans weren't here, we are toxic destroying everything, even ourselves.

On the 16th of November 2022, a bomb landed on a village farm in Poland and killed two farmers. Poland is in NATO and the warning to Putin from NATO was not to cross the line into other European countries after his aggression in Ukraine. This was the warning that if any bombs entered another country other than Ukraine there would be repercussions, meaning his country would be bombed.

On the 17th of November 2022, we were waiting for information following the inspection of the bomb to know how it got there. I think we knew where it came from, but it could have been a Ukrainian missile sent to explode the Russian missile and that landed in Poland. We didn't know but it was worrying because if it wasn't a mistake or a defending missile, that meant Putin intended it to land in Poland and that could mean a war, probably a world war at that.

Eventually the result was that the bomb was a defending missile from Ukraine. I think there must have been a massive sigh of relief from the world! It was winter and getting colder in the UK but in Ukraine the snow had already fallen and the temperature had dropped and the Ukrainians were freezing. Putin had blown up their electric grid and cut the power off, what an evil bastard. We heard from Ukrainian survivors about the awful evil war crimes that had been going on for months and that the Russian soldiers' wives were telling them to rape the Ukrainian women and children. If that was true what kind of people are the Russians? If their women think like that then they are as bad as their men. Russians appear to be monsters in human form, no decent people would do the monstrous things the Russians have done and continue to do.

Christmas was almost on us and we'd go through the process, put the tree up and have Christmas dinner and that's about it, we still couldn't be bothered with Christmas, so we didn't bother. Mum got her dementia clock, which is helping, but she is forgetting to look at it sometimes and still asking me what day it is, so now I'm telling her to look at her clock. New Year came and went quietly, nothing new there then. New Year was nothing like it used to be. People would spend most of Hogmanay preparing food and drink and cleaning the house for all the people that would be coming in after the bells - that was what happened at New Year. You would visit relatives and friends through the night to eat and drink, end up pissed and either make it home or just fall asleep where you ended up.

Happy New Year seemed an odd thing to say because I think we knew it was not going to be happy or prosperous for many of us, but we still said it to each other. It was 2023 and I couldn't see the year being any better than the past three. One good thing was that I had a pretty good wage rise so that would help us out. Shaila had finally won her three-year case against the social, and they have decided now that she was too ill to work again. This was extremely good news as she couldn't even do housework without getting really sore between her back and her hips. She was really suffering, and the cysts were destroying her body too. She's got a lot going on and is in acute pain every day.

The social department decided that she was to get the money backdated a couple of years to when she put in the first claim. She was to get £4000 and her monthly invalidity money increased to the highest payment. This was really good news- we could buy a car.

It was the end of January now. We went down to the car sales place in Dalkeith to look at cars and immediately saw one for six and a half grand. The sales guy came out and we said we liked that one. We looked inside; it was quite a big car with a few good features like a good-sized boot. Shaila said she liked it, so we went in and bought it. She paid three grand, and I put in the rest from the rent money that she would get back monthly now that she had a bit more money coming in. We decided to help Stuart set up a new business doing his joinery and DIY jobs. He would do the main things on the jobs, and we would do his bookkeeping, answering the phone, cleaning up after big jobs, and helping him in any way we could.

We still didn't have our own place to live, we were still cramped up in our small house, so our aim was to stop wasting money and start making as much as we could. If you are reading this book, you're helping us to a better life and you're also helping women's charities such as Refuge and Women's Aid as I'm giving 20% of the proceeds from this book to them forever.

All our birthdays had passed and we were into February. I was now 58, Shaila was 56, and Cameron 54 — another year closer to death. What more could one want?

The government was still in a deadlock with the nurses, train workers, teachers and other public sectors, so strikes were still ongoing and they would become more intense and prolonged. The government needed to back down as this was harming the economy even more. So, at the start of 2023. Job opportunities were coming in for Stuart and for once, we had reliable transport. I was applying to the domestic department for weekend work as soon as I heard they were looking for staff. I've had enough of sick people and their unhappy relatives. I'm sick of being a packhorse on the ward. I was pissed off with lazy nurses. There's a level of neglect by nurses as a result of that laziness. The bottom line is most nursing staff don't want to touch a patient, they don't want to wash people, help them to the toilet or clean people that have been incontinent. This is a big problem because people are being left to hold on to go to the toilet or left lying in their piss and mess until a Health Care Assistant, like me, is free to do it. This is not right. Why are three or four people allocated to look after twelve patients not enough? It *is* enough, but only one of us does the majority of the physical work with the patients. That hurts patients and support staff. When you get asked questions by patients and relatives like, 'Are you the only one on?' or 'Do the nurses help at all?', it's not good. All staff are supposed to be there for the patients, but they are not. Some are there for the money or for the glory of being a nurse, or the fact that they have power over a person all day (a Health Care Assis). A lot of them like that.

The NHS NEEDS TO BE REFORMED. First, they need to get to grips with the budget. The wastage in the NHS is immense — from food to drugs that get thrown out. or the laundry, which must take a big chunk of the budget. When I was trained, we were told to replenish sheets if we could. They told us to take the bottom sheet off and then put the top sheet on the bottom, providing the top sheet was still clean, and put a clean sheet on the top. That way, only one sheet was being put in for the wash per day, which makes total sense. But of course, rather than do what they are supposed to, some nursing staff think it's okay to change the sheets whether they are dirty or not. This is only one example of people doing what they want in the NHS. Who's there to stop them? The answer is no one.

February arrived. Nothing much to report that month except Stuart and Derry announced they were pregnant. That was a shocker. Not only were they pregnant, but they were also expecting twins. OMG, I almost had a heart attack. Luckily, I was already sitting down. That's a double shock for me. I never thought Stuart would want any kids, but they both seemed to be over the moon. Putin was still killing innocent people in Ukraine. The cost of living was still ridiculously high. Electricity cost us £300 a month for 5 people, not including the gas, which was around £50 if we were very careful. The food shopping was around £400 a month. It used to be around £200. So, as you can see, around £350, alone. And then you've got the internet, the bus fares, the council tax going up, up, up. Everything you went to do or buy was costing double.

March 2023 was a bit better. The lighter nights and mornings were coming back. That's when you know the weather will get better, and spring is on the way. I also had some good news from a friend of mine who was in the hospital's domestic department. She told me that her domestic department was looking for weekend cleaning staff. I asked her to get me an application form and she brought it to me that afternoon. I was so grateful to her as this could be the start of a new job that I was sure I'd like better than the one I did, a lot less stress and only one boss. No more having to bow down to people who think they are better than me.

I put the application in and asked the universe to help me get an interview. Two weeks passed, and I was starting to worry that they weren't going to give me an interview where I could persuade them to give me a job. Two or three days later, I got a phone call asking me if I would like to come in for an interview, and of course, I said yes. It went well. Two days later, they phoned me to offer me the job. I had done it. What a relief. I don't suppose you would see someone as happy as me to get a cleaning job, but for the record, I like cleaning, I was a cleaner before I went into nursing. The hospital needed to be cleaned, and it's human beings that do it, just like it's human beings that do almost everything on this planet. No one is any better than anyone else; we just do different things to survive because that's what life is — survival.

I was to start my new job on 1st April. I was there bright and early at 7 o'clock. My hours are 7 till 3, Saturday and Sunday contracted hours, but I would be able to make up full-time hours once April was over. The first weekend was a bit strange. I was in the same hospital but doing a different job. I was cleaning people's arses and other bits now I was cleaning the environment around them. I didn't have to touch or smell another human being again. All I can say is thank goodness. I wouldn't miss it. I could still speak to the patients, so that's good enough for me now.

My second weekend doing the cleaning was a bit more familiar. I was put in a ward I knew well, I had worked there many times. I was to clean it by myself. I thought, fair enough. I worked extremely hard and cleaned the whole ward. I was knackered at the end of the shift, but I'd completed the challenge, which was so satisfying.

It was so good going in and not being pressured by others all day. My stress levels had gone from very high to very low. I now only had one boss, not several. I could just get on with my job without any hassle. As long as I did my work, the supervisors didn't bother me. It was a much more relaxed atmosphere among the domestics. No one thought they were the big 'I am' we were all equal, which made work far more bearable. It's been the right move for me. The third and fourth weekends were a bit easier as I was putting my cleaning skills into action. The ward staff noticed I had changed jobs and many asked me why. I just said simply, I had enough of nursing and all the nonsense that goes with it, so I decided to get out when there was an opportunity. Some said, 'Who can blame you?' and others said that was fair enough.

My supervisor was happy with me. She put in a good word with the head manager, saying I was doing great, no problems with my work or timekeeping. I was happy with that. I don't particularly want to be a cleaner; it's hard going for a 58-year-old, but so was the support nursing that did my head in, as well as my body. I hoped it was only a stepping stone to retirement. You never know; this book might bring me enough money to retire in a couple of years. I'm praying that's what will happen. Maybe family problems will have gone by that time and we can have some peace in our lives.

I kind of got used to the idea that I was probably going to be a domestic until I retired. Then I got a message from Shaila saying one of her old school friends was selling her snack van for 8 grand; she said it was a little gold mine. I thought we could go and have a look at it. We arranged a day, but she cancelled. Then we arranged another day, and the same happened. We had given up and then she got in touch a couple of weeks later, saying she had got her act together if we still wanted to come and see it. We thought we might as well. It was quite a good deal; the van had everything we needed. It was a little rusty on one of the sides, but it was in pretty good condition.

We thought about it overnight. I was a bit scared because that would be another 8 grand wasted if it didn't succeed, but we'd been looking to open something up here. Shaila said if we keep just thinking about things, we'll get nowhere. So I thought, what the hell, why not? I really needed to change my job anyway, so why not a snack van? I started thinking it might be quite good if we went to festivals. With the atmosphere, it wouldn't feel like work, and we could do as we pleased. We would need to get a pitch somewhere as well, to have weekly money coming in. The owner of the van gave us the woman's number that she hired her pitch from, so hopefully, she will hire it out to us next. The next day, we talked about it and decided to take it, in the hope we would get the weekly pitch. Now I'm going to have to come up with some amazing food for a reasonable price. I still hated cooking, but maybe if I was getting paid to do it, it might be different. I didn't think it could be as physically exhausting as what I was doing, and that was very appealing to me.

The van needed a good clean. We've had to make a driveway in the front garden to park it as it needs to be plugged in at night, it had a fridge freezer in it and a battery that needed to be kept charged. Stuart did the driveway and did a really good job of it. Now we could bring the van home and start cleaning it and applying for permits and stuff. Who knows if this would work? Only time would tell, but we'd try our hardest to make a living, if nothing else.

In the summer of July 2023. OMG, what the hell was starting to unfold was unbelievable. Greece, Spain and Portugal were burning in over 40-degree temperatures. A couple of countries on the other side of the world were flooding and of course, this was put down to global warming. A few days later, fires were out, but it created devastation. A lot of homes were burnt to the ground, and wildlife was destroyed. The weather in the UK was awful. June was a great month, but July was dull, wet and a bit cold at times, and as we came into August, it was not much better in Britain. I was thinking what a rubbish summer, and then I heard on the news that the beautiful island of Hawaii was now burning. There were a few outbursts of wildfires in the States with Death Valley hitting almost 50 degrees. It was looking very bad for Hawaii; the fire was ripping it up very quickly and people were running for their lives. This went on for days; it destroyed everything in its path. They finally got it to stop and then we saw the devastation in Maui. It's decimated 80% of the town of Lahaina. All the wildlife had gone, people's pets were gone, loved ones too. The death toll reached 101 but there were about a thousand people not accounted for. This was the worst wildfire yet. It was like they had been transported to hell. One woman said all she could see was smoke and people screaming and crying and car horns going off. Some people made it to the sea and were in there for hours, one family were in the water for 15 hours and all they wanted to do was sleep, but they couldn't, they had to keep finding ways of staying awake. This has to be the worst consequence of ignoring the warnings we have had for years about global warming. Well, here we are, all you people who haven't done anything to help the situation, well done. Your kids and everything you love will be destroyed in the future, once again, thank God I didn't have kids.

The wildfires eventually went out. They had caused massive destruction that would take years to fix. It was the end of August and it wouldn't be long till the twins were born. Derry was struggling now with them, it must be hard having two humans living in your stomach, growing by the day, getting bigger and bigger, moving and kicking you. That's my idea of hell. I just think I would panic if I had a human growing in me, I would just want it out. In September 2023, I thought it was time to wrap this book up and finish it. There wasn't much more to say, nothing much was happening, just the same old stuff and then Derry started to be very ill with vomiting and they noticed the little girl wasn't growing the same as the boy.

Derry had to go twice a week to be monitored by the antenatal clinic to make sure the baby girl was getting enough food and maintaining her growth. They were a bit worried about her and then near the end of September, Derry was constantly throwing up, so they admitted her and gave her fluids and anti-sickness. She was exhausted. It was time for them to come out, so a few days later, they were born by Caesarean. The little girl, called Ella May, and the boy called Leo. Ella -May was tiny. Leo was a bit bigger but both were premature by nearly 4 weeks. They had to go into the incubators as they were premature. Stuart and Derry practically lived in the hospital to be close to their twins. Stuart did a lot of running about, he was showing real fatherly qualities. He really loved his twins and was stepping up to the mark. It was coming to the end of the month when Leo was discharged, but Ella May had to stay another few days. The day finally came for Ella May to go home, I think it was close to 31st October as that was her original due date.

Chapter Eighteeen

October 7th - A very bad day 2023

October 7th, 2023 could be viewed as the beginning of the end for us all. Hamas, who are a Palestinian terror organisation, were voted in by threatening the Palestinian people to vote for them. They took the massive decision to rip down the fencing at the Gaza border between Israel and Palestine and start shooting Jewish teenagers who were enjoying an open-air concert. They were on motorbikes and cars storming in, shooting and grabbing people to take as hostages. They took old women, young children from neighbouring villages and teenagers from the concert. It was a terrible thing to watch. This was planned, and it was done quickly. Of course, this enraged the Israelis. They took revenge in a big way and started bombing Palestine and the defenceless people living there. This caused a final break to an already delicate situation- it was all-out war now between them. Israel said they were going to kill the Hamas terrorists bombing the Gaza Strip to bits claiming that the terrorists were operating from tunnels underneath schools, apartment blocks and hospitals. The massive problem with that was that there were thousands of civilians there. That didn't matter to them; they bombed the place bit by bit, killing men, women and children and injuring thousands of people every day. It was disgusting to see how those people were suffering. They were not Hamas; they were civilians. Most of them hated the Hamas group, so why should they suffer like this? They've no food except for the little drizzles of aid that get through the border from Egypt.

So here was another war. It shouldn't really be called a war because a war consists of two sides fighting it out, but this was one side attacking unarmed people who were just living their already difficult lives. The Israelis can deny they have been killing innocent people, evicting people from their homes and demolishing homes in Gaza for years now, but they can't deny they control the power and water supply for the region. What I want to know is why was Israel allowed to control these supplies? It's not right. Who do they think they are? This should not happen to any country. I'm sorry, but I can see why the Palestinians hate the Israelis, but I'm struggling to see why the Israelis hate the Palestinians. The Israelis want to kill all the Hamas members, but at the same time, they're killing ordinary people. They're wiping out complete families; they're leaving thousands of children alone and injured after their parents have been slaughtered. Medical staff are exhausted, working 24/7 with hardly any food or water. What will happen when they can't go on any longer?

It was and still is a terrible time. Palestine was just a massive graveyard. Where would it end? When they'd killed all the Hamas fighters and most of the population as well? Some countries called for a ceasefire to let aid in and help the injured, but no, the Israelis said no ceasefire. It really was hell on earth, and the world was allowing it to happen. The Israelis who were killed and taken hostage were innocent people, and so are the Palestinian people who did nothing to hurt anyone that day, yet it was ok to do this to them. They are as innocent as the Israelis that day, but yet they're being wiped out. It's starting to look a lot like what the Germans did to the Jews but in a different way, which makes them just as bad as the Germans.

Some people may not like me saying that, so let's strip it down. The Jews were persecuted and executed by a madman and his cronies. They were helpless and defenceless ordinary people just living their lives, and the next thing, they were being slaughtered. Does this ring any alarm bells? The bells are saying to me it's very similar situation, but in Gaza, death is very slow for some who are lying injured, starving and dehydrated. This has to be the worst situation any human can be in, and yet there are thousands of women, children, and old people needing help, lying with legs and arms blown off, bleeding to death. I can't believe I've just written that, but unfortunately, humans have hardly learnt a thing over the years about why wars shouldn't happen. What I just wrote was happening in 2023. I'm sure things weren't meant to be this way when we were created, but we've made our planet a horrible, unsafe, shitty place to grow up in, live through, and die through, for millions of us.

By April 2nd, 2024, the Israelis were still killing and starving the Palestinians. They bombed a charity that was travelling to Gaza in vans with food and other supplies. The convoy was cleared by the Israeli authorities to go to Gaza, but was attacked with drones from above, killing the aid workers and destroying the vital aid people needed. What kind of monster is Netanyahu? He had just had a hernia operation in a clean, safe environment, and probably had the best food and two nights in peace to think over what he's done. Is he all right with killing kids and defenceless women and men, blowing people to bits, blowing limbs off children, women, and men who are just left to bleed to death? And those that are saved, what aftercare do they have? Probably very little to none. People who lose limbs need time to adapt, learn how to get by with what they have left, and come to terms with what they've lost. They need good nutrition, pain relief, antibiotics and somewhere to recover. I just want people to think about what these people are going through. They don't just suffer blown-off limbs. What about burns and shrapnel injuries on top of the mental trauma they're suffering?

Chapter Nineteen
Summing Up – A Word to the Wise 2023

If you're reading this page in this last chapter, it should mean that you've read my story and now you've reached the end unless you're one of these people that read the end first, which is weird, but each to their own. Thank you for taking the time to read this book. I hope you've enjoyed it and learnt something from it. Also, if you've paid for the book, you are also helping the women's refuge centres - a huge thank you for that.

So, I've called my last chapter summing up - a summary of an ordinary family with an unordinary life. After the childhood I endured, I believe that any woman or any man who finds themselves in a volatile relationship should get out after the first signs, whether it's a slap, a push, an unnecessary angry reply, being told what to wear or eat or anything designed to make them feel small. You shouldn't have feelings like that. Alarm bells should ring, but very often they don't, so if you feel things aren't right, trust yourself, you're probably right. Other people in your life shouldn't be allowed to make you feel bad - as I always say if there's something rotten in your fridge, get rid of it!

I know that these control freaks will have already got into your heart and your head, until the day comes when the first offence is committed and there's no more Mr Nice Guy, just sorrow, fear, and anxiety to come from then on. I think it's plain to see what your life with a monster will be like and then if kids are involved it's a whole new kettle of fish to boil as you worry about them as well. It is not a good situation.

I'm sure I've said before that domestic abuse is the name given for what is really going on and that is assault and battery, coercive control and rape. These are all against the law but it still goes on and it still is going on today, unbelievably so. The help we had was practically none, but now there is help and women are being saved, but anyone suffering will need to make the first step to ask for help. Please don't wait until you're broken and helpless. As long as they have you in their control, you don't stand a chance. You need others to help you get rid of the bad rubbish. I know it's not easy and sometimes people might get hurt or even killed, but when you're in a volatile situation these things could very well happen anyway, at any time. Most bullies are cowards when it comes down to it. Some will back down and go away quicker than others, some might create holy hell before they go and unfortunately, some will kill for revenge. Abusers are full of hate and hate breeds hate. It can be passed on to your kids, and I'm sure most women don't want their kids to be abusers or suffer mentally because of what they heard and saw.

So that's my advice: leave early when things seem to be changing for the worst. You must plan it though, don't stay and let this person ruin you and your kids' lives.

Bullying

Moving on to bullying, it's not a good thing, not for the recipient anyway. I think with childhood bullying, kids usually have a reason for doing it. It could be because you fell out with someone and they didn't like it, or you anymore. In my case, they started it because I was good-looking and slim and receiving all the attention at the disco. They didn't like that so they decided to do something about it. I think some kids really enjoy it; they don't seem to care at all what they are putting another child through. It's all for laughs as well. Kids like an audience; most of them are proud of what they are doing. They like to be known as someone who is not scared to go after another, so, therefore, they must be feared.

If I had a kid who was bullying another child, I think I would be devastated that my son or daughter could make someone else's life a misery. I don't know if bullies are brought up differently to other kids, I suspect some of them are. Where else will they learn this behaviour? Some of it might come from TV and the internet, but either way, it doesn't matter because it's wrong as we know, but it still goes on unfortunately.

Now a word or two about adult bullying. Adult bullies know what they are doing. Some people use authority to bring the bully out, some use words and others use actions. Adult bullies, just like kids, don't give a shit about how they're dissolving people's lives into dust. Some people are already getting bullied at home, they don't need another idiot doing it outside the home, wherever it might be happening.

Some bullies get their comeuppance. My bully is now dead at 58 years old. She had undergone a transplant; I'm not sure what organ it was. She was in intensive care but she died. I was shocked. I wouldn't have wanted that for her, but sometimes karma does catch up with us.

Holidays

First of all, if you're going camping, don't lose the tent poles or run out of money. Don't go away with strangers for any reason. We were lucky, we managed to get enough to eat until we got home and a roof over our heads, on our French adventure but it could have been a life-or-death situation because we didn't know the man who was helping us (for a price) but yet we went with him, I went twice to his apartment. This was a very stupid and dangerous thing to do, but we lived to tell the tale.

Don't go on holiday with hotheads - they can go off at any time for any reason or no reason at all. They can get themselves in trouble and the people they are with. Holidays are for relaxation and happiness, not stress and disorder.

Relationships

Don't fall in love with losers no matter how much you have the hots for them. A good partner should be working, able to understand they are not above or below you, they are equal to you and any other female. They don't own you or possess you. A partner has to recognise that he or she is responsible for their own mess. They must help with household duties as well. They should not be selfish, greedy, violent or aggressive and must love animals. I don't think it's too much to ask for because this is how I live my life and don't find it hard to be kind, thoughtful, generous and hardworking, so why would I want any less from others?

You may be a woman, but that means no less than a man. Most men are idiots anyway, so in reality world, women are far better people and they are the ones that grow and produce life. A man just makes it happen by doing something they love anyway, having sex. That's what most men have at the top of their list, above everything else. If men told the truth about themselves, everyone would know where they stand.

If you're married the same applies. The ring on the finger and the ceremony is only a symbol of trust and faithfulness and even then it all gets binned when one of you is unfaithful. I don't believe in marriage, what's the point of it? Most people end up divorced. I don't think humans were supposed to stay with the same partner for life; I think the history of relationships proves this, so don't think because you're married you're safe. Most men don't tell you what they're thinking. Why is that? It's because if they were to be really truthful you wouldn't like what they were thinking. May I add this does not include the small amount of men in the world who do reveal their true selves and are kind and considerate. They're rare and if you've got one, hold on to him!

Money

The love of money is the root of all evil, the Bible tells us. One day someone, somewhere decided that things shouldn't be free anymore, so that person discussed it with other men (let's face it, it would have been men that invented money). It will be recorded who invented it and when and how and why. I could look it up but I just can't be bothered.

So, money was invented which is ok if you were someone who had it, but if you don't have much, not enough or worst-case scenario, none, that's a different story, and not a good one. If you have a few thousand, don't waste it. The love of money might be the root of all evil, but you need it, and in this day and age, a lot of it. When you get your hands on it, hold on to it if you can, certainly don't waste it, as we have done.

Money should not define you. Why are most of the rich, nasty shits? Because they can be. Money can buy anything, except a get-out-of-jail card, so the rich can do what they want as long as they don't get caught breaking the law.

One of my school friend's brothers started his business majoring on criminality; he's loaded! Now, they say it doesn't pay to be a criminal, but in some cases, if you don't get caught, it does pay very good money. The other day I heard on the news that robberies are on the rise, especially house robberies where the police can't do much. With no witnesses, they don't know who did it and have no way of finding out either, so burglars just get away with it.

The Rich/Poor Divide

On the 29th of June 2023 I watched Good Morning Britain and the discussion was about how a poor woman took her life because of the despair she was experiencing at the hands of the authorities. She was on benefits and was put into a house that wasn't suitable for a dog, yet the authorities thought it was okay to put a human being into a damp place, crumbling to bits and where a part of the ceiling had fallen into her room. The housing company knew the state of the place but did nothing to help her. They added to the stress saying she owed them money that was overpaid to her, so once again they were trying to get blood out of a stone. This is what they do, they make mistakes, and it's the claimant who suffers. Generally, people on benefits don't have extra money to pay back the social for their mistakes.

I know this happens. The benefits office make mistakes and then blames it on the down-and-out person who's already had enough and is on the brink of doing something drastic. This has happened to my family and a couple of my friends. They say you owe them and they will take it back from the pittances you already get from the government. In this woman's case, they tortured her with all that and then put her into a house that was falling to bits. How the hell is that helping her? All the agencies she went to for help either couldn't or wouldn't help her. What are they there for then?

So the despair became too much and believed that the only way out was to take her life. She thought she was fighting a losing battle, and she was right. There is no help for a person who's got NO money. Oh, what a bloody surprise. Surely that's the opposite way around; shouldn't she be the one getting free things thrown at her? Because we all know that the rich get things free, simply because they're well-off.

To be honest, I can't see that much has changed since the slave trade; we still have slaves of all colours. It's a social thing now. I call myself a poorly paid slave because that's how I feel, and many others feel that way too. I think there is a change coming; every other prejudice has been tackled, so now it's time for this to get sorted out.

The Final Page - September 2023

We have arrived at the final page. Not many people write a book. I would say it's not easy, even when you know the story. If you're making it up, that's even harder; it's a lot of brain work. Summer is over, and autumn is here once again; another year has just whizzed by.

Things weren't supposed to work out like this. My plan was to be retired by now in my own place, abroad somewhere. I've decided that I'm probably not going to be living abroad now, so I'll just have to make the most of life here. We bought the snack van but haven't done anything with it so far. I'm thinking that we made a mistake buying it, but I need to change what I do and soon. Maybe we'll have to give it a go now or sell it and probably lose some more money.

I think I'm probably going to move from here to a place called Musselburgh. Mum and I would be a lot happier there, we already like it there. It's a nice little town; it has a river running through it with swans and ducks in it. It has a harbour and it's near to the sea, which is where I've always wanted to be. Also, it's got good shops and takeaways within walking distance or a short bus journey away. It has a few shops like pound shops and the supermarket, cafes, restaurants, and the famous Lucas ice cream shop. It has a better bus service than I have now, as well.

I don't think I'll learn to drive at this stage and I can't rely on other people to drive me, so I need somewhere that I can access anything I need. I suppose this will have to be the plan if this book doesn't succeed because this is the last thing I can try to get us a better life. It's already been a lifetime for me as I'm almost 59, and time's running out for us. Getting old comes quicker every year; I just want to live whatever time I have left in peace. I also want to enjoy life for a change and I want Mum to have more than what she's got. She's wasting away in boredom, and everyone seems to be fine with that because it's easier than taking her somewhere. And those in the States think it's okay to ignore what's going on over here and leave it all to us. I think there will be some regrets there.

I hope you've enjoyed reading our story and maybe learned something too as I will pledge a percentage to the Womens Charities of my Royalties after I have had my few thousand back first. I hope to make a few bob with this book and I hope it could be a drama or a film because there is so much not written in this book as it would have cost more and I couldn't pay for a longer book on top of everything else I have to pay for, but watch this space as I never give up, hopefully it will become a film or a drama or maybe a second book, the public and the universe will decide I suppose.

So the story I gave you was from an ordinary family with a very unordinary life. I hope you enjoyed it.

The End

www.ingramcontent.com/pod-product-compliance
Lightning Source LLC
Chambersburg PA
CBHW071157070526
44584CB00019B/2832